EASY GUITAR WITH NOTES & TAB

2nd EDITION

VERY BEST OF COLDPLAY

T0116620

ISBN 978-1-4950-9011-0

7777 W. BLUEMOUND RD. P.O. BOX 13819 MILWAUKEE, WI 53213

In Australia Contact:
Hal Leonard Australia Pty. Ltd.
4 Lentara Court
Cheltenham, Victoria, 3192 Australia
Email: ausadmin@halleonard.com.au

For all works contained herein:
Unauthorized copying, arranging, adapting, recording, Internet posting, public performance,
or other distribution of the printed music in this publication is an infringement of copyright.
Infringers are liable under the law.

Visit Hal Leonard Online at
www.halleonard.com

STRUM AND PICK PATTERNS

This chart contains the suggested strum and pick patterns that are referred to by number at the beginning of each song in this book. The symbols ⊓ and ∨ in the strum patterns refer to down and up strokes, respectively. The letters in the pick patterns indicate which right-hand fingers play which strings.

p = thumb
i = index finger
m = middle finger
a = ring finger

For example; Pick Pattern 2
is played: thumb - index - middle - ring

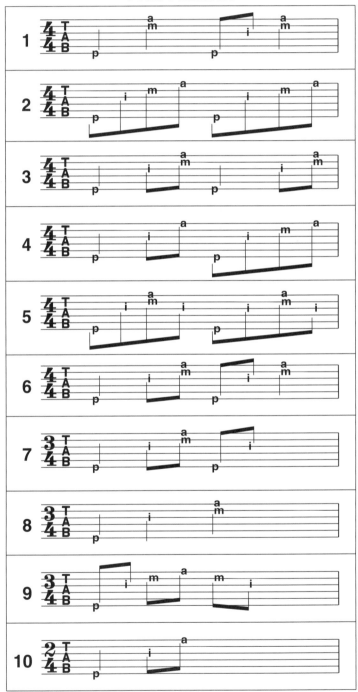

Strum Patterns   **Pick Patterns**

You can use the 3/4 Strum and Pick Patterns in songs written in compound meter (6/8, 9/8, 12/8, etc.). For example, you can accompany a song in 6/8 by playing the 3/4 pattern twice in each measure. The 4/4 Strum and Pick Patterns can be used for songs written in cut time (¢) by doubling the note time values in the patterns. Each pattern would therefore last two measures in cut time.

CONTENTS

Adventure of a Lifetime

**Words and Music by Guy Berryman, Jon Buckland, Chris Martin,
Will Champion, Mikkel Eriksen and Tor Hermansen**

*1st time, N.C., next 4 meas.

Copyright © 2015 by Universal Music Publishing MGB Ltd. and EMI Music Publishing Ltd.
All Rights for Universal Music Publishing MGB Ltd. in the United States and Canada Administered by Universal Music - MGB Songs
All Rights for EMI Music Publishing Ltd. Administered by
Sony/ATV Music Publishing LLC, 424 Church Street, Suite 1200, Nashville, TN 37219
International Copyright Secured   All Rights Reserved

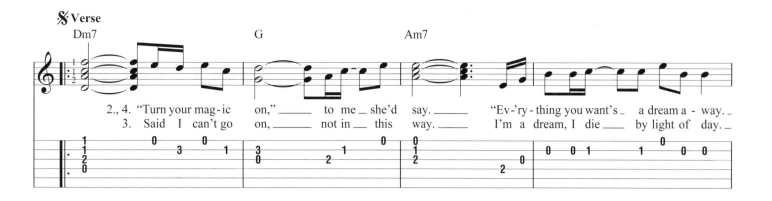

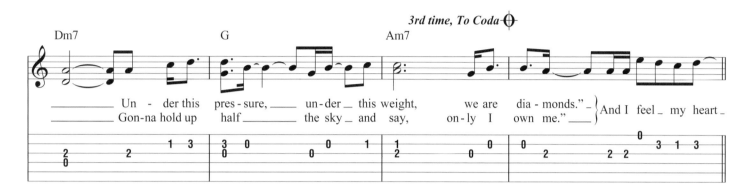

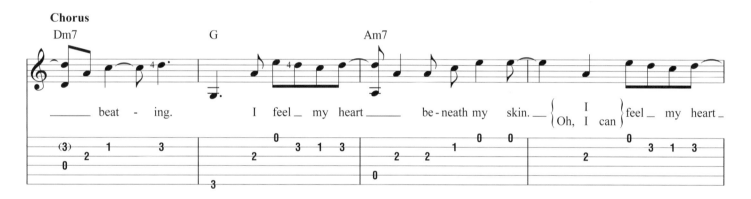

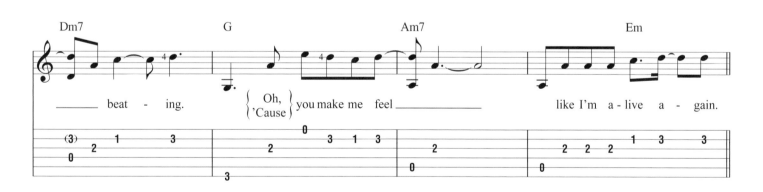

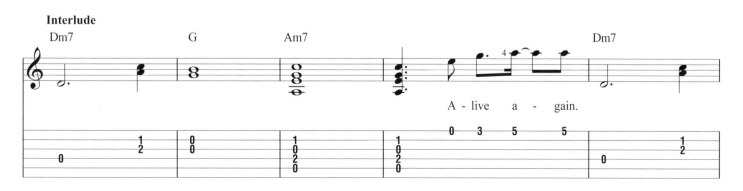

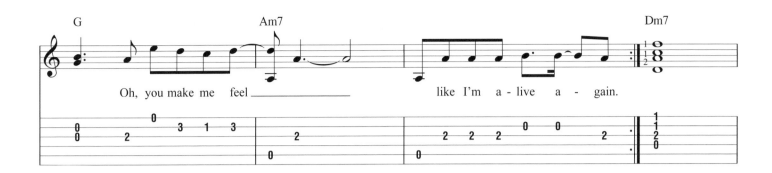

Oh, you make me feel _____ like I'm a-live a - gain.

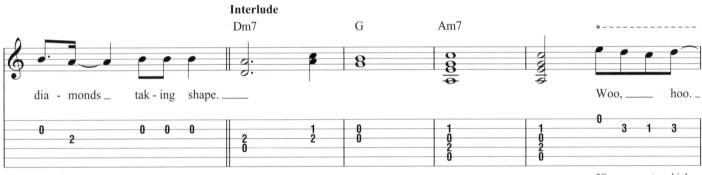

D.S. al Coda

⊕ **Coda**

dia - monds _ tak - ing shape, _____ we are

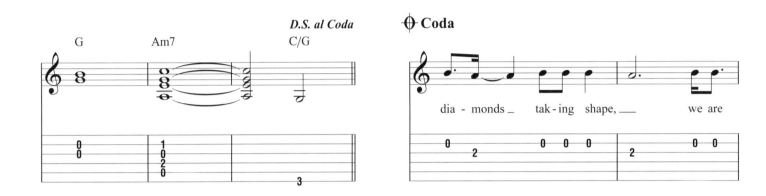

Interlude

dia - monds _ tak - ing shape. _____ Woo, _____ hoo. _

*Sung one octave higher.

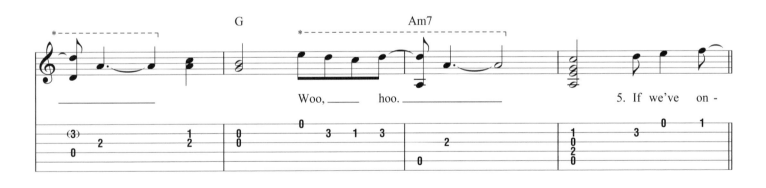

Woo, _____ hoo. _____ 5. If we've on -

Verse

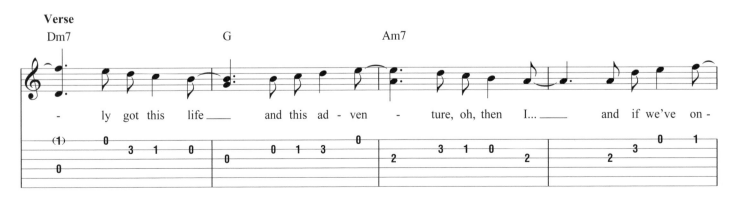

- ly got this life _____ and this ad - ven - ture, oh, then I... _____ and if we've on -

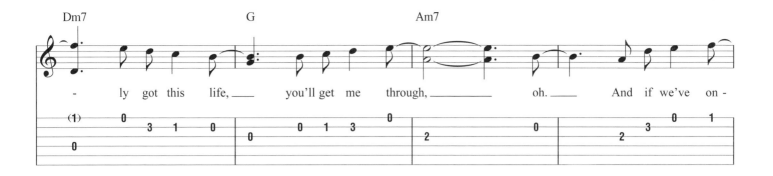

-ly got this life, ___ you'll get me through, ___ oh. ___ And if we've on-

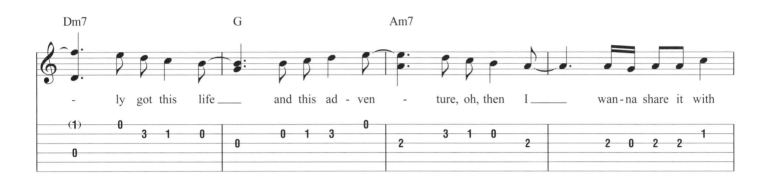

-ly got this life ___ and this ad - ven - ture, oh, then I ___ wan-na share it with

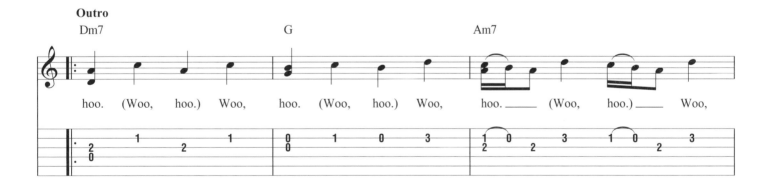

you, with you, with you. ___ Sing it, oh, ___ sing, yeah. Woo,

*Sung one octave higher.

Outro

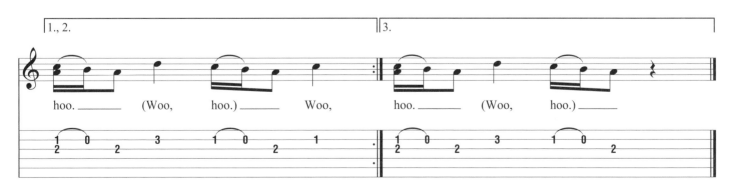

hoo. (Woo, hoo.) Woo, hoo. (Woo, hoo.) Woo, hoo. ___ (Woo, hoo.) ___ Woo,

1., 2.

hoo. ___ (Woo, hoo.) ___ Woo,

3.

hoo. ___ (Woo, hoo.) ___

Clocks

Words and Music by Guy Berryman, Jon Buckland, Will Champion and Chris Martin

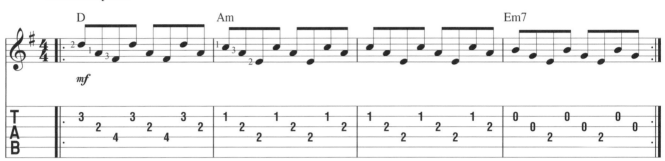

Strum Pattern: 1, 5
Pick Pattern: 2, 4

Intro
Moderately fast

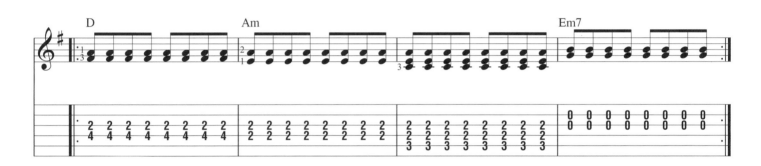

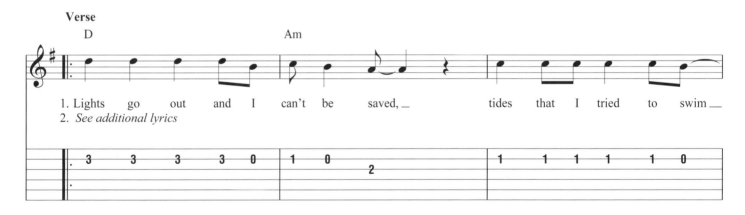

Verse

1. Lights go out and I can't be saved, ___ tides that I tried to swim ___
2. *See additional lyrics*

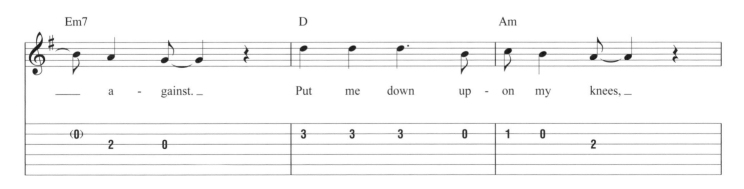

___ a - gainst. ___ Put me down up - on my knees, ___

Copyright © 2002 by Universal Music Publishing MGB Ltd.
All Rights in the United States Administered by Universal Music - MGB Songs
International Copyright Secured   All Rights Reserved

oh, I beg, I beg and plead. __ Sing - in': come out with

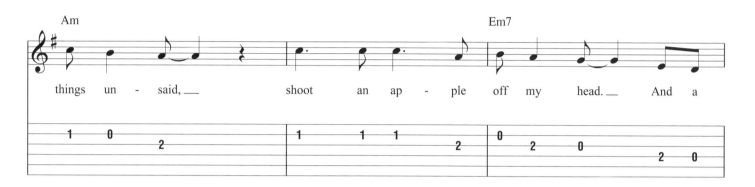

things un - said, __ shoot an ap - ple off my head. __ And a

trou - ble that can't be named, __ a ti - ger's wait - ing

Chorus

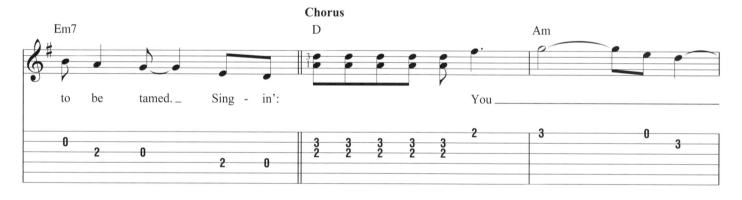

to be tamed. __ Sing - in': You __

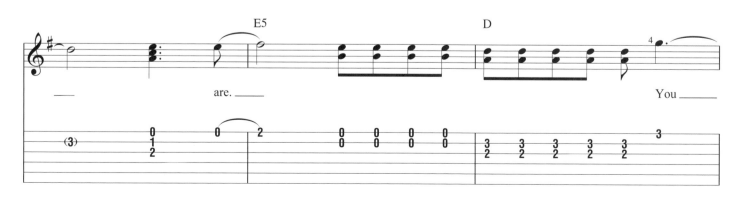

__ are. __ You __

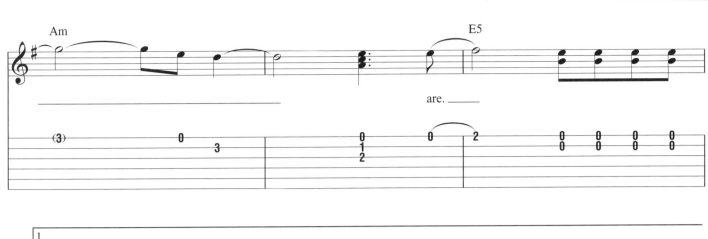

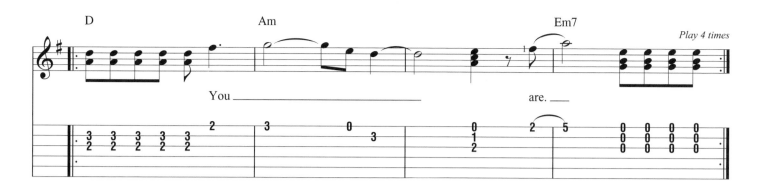

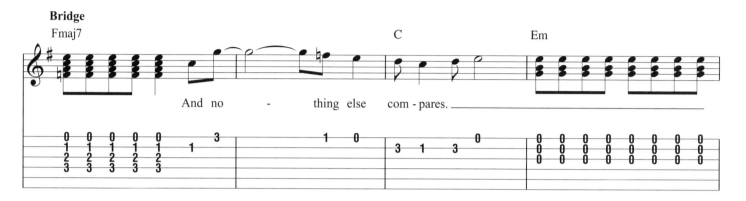

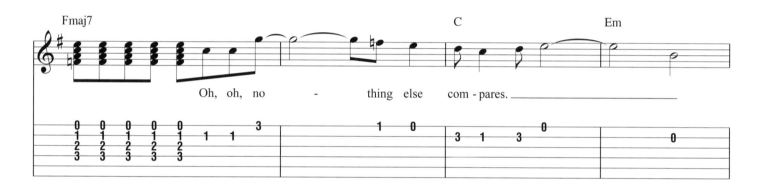

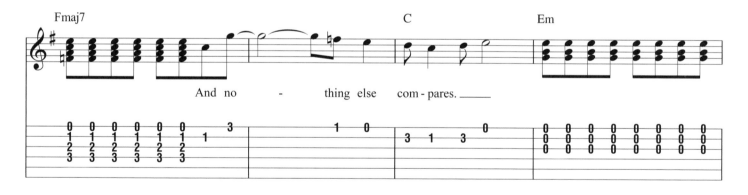

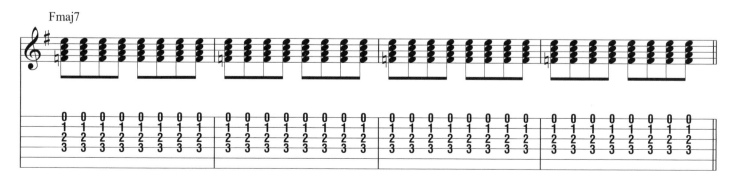

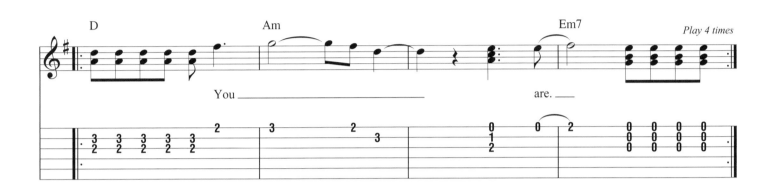

You _____ are. ___

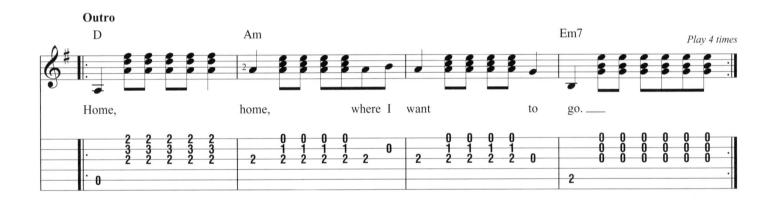

Outro

Home,   home,   where I want   to   go. ___

Repeat and fade

Additional Lyrics

2. Confusion that never stops, closing walls and tickin' clocks.
   Gonna come back and take you home, I could not stop, that you now know.
   Singin': come out upon my seas, cursed missed opportunities.
   Am I a part of the cure, or am I part of the disease?

Green Eyes

Words and Music by Guy Berryman, Jon Buckland, Will Champion and Chris Martin

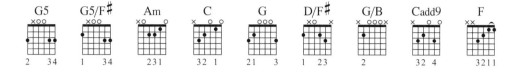

*Capo II
Strum Pattern: 3
Pick Pattern: 4

*Optional: To match recording, place capo at 2nd fret.

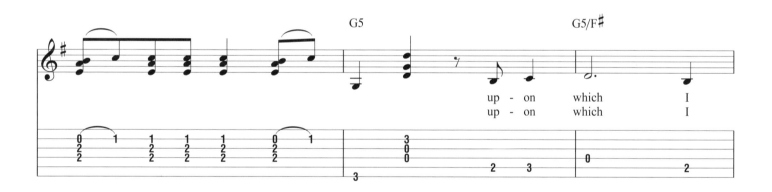

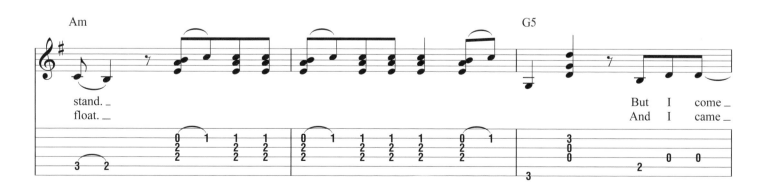

Copyright © 2002 by Universal Music Publishing MGB Ltd.
All Rights in the United States Administered by Universal Music - MGB Songs
International Copyright Secured   All Rights Reserved

Pre-Chorus

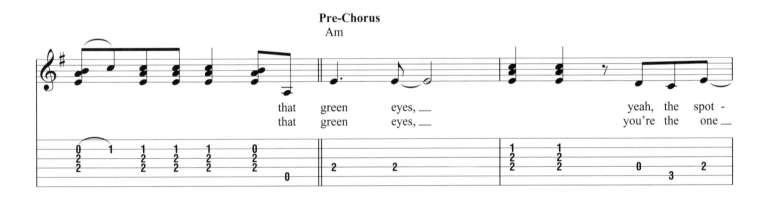

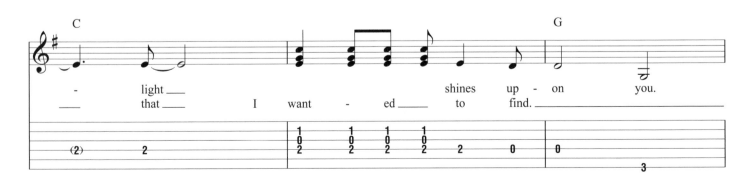

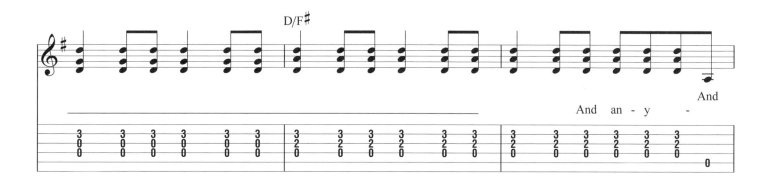

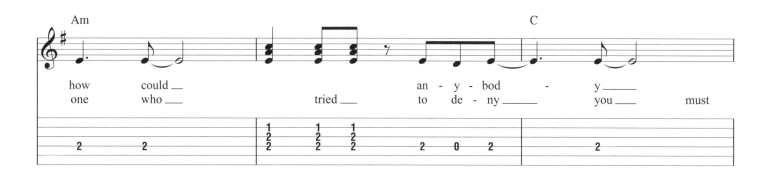

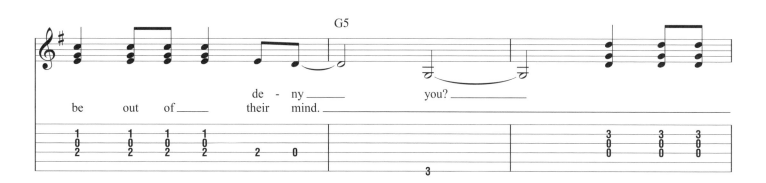

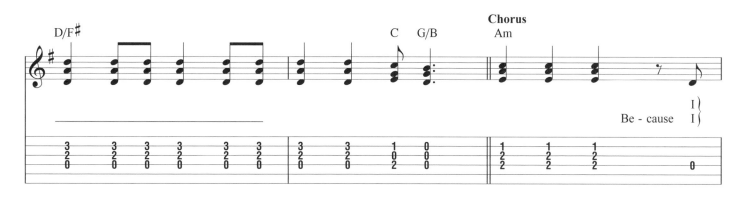

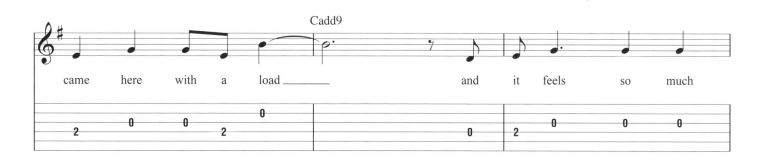

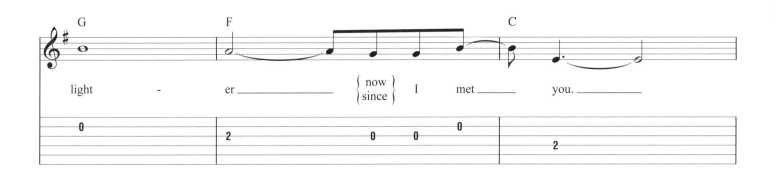

light - er _____ { now / since } I met _____ you. _____

And, hon - ey, you should know _____

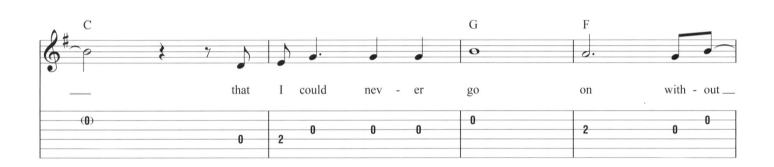

that I could nev - er go on with - out _____

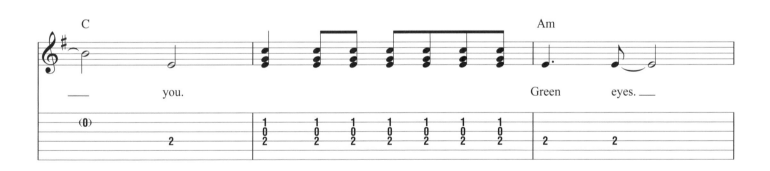

_____ you. Green eyes. _____

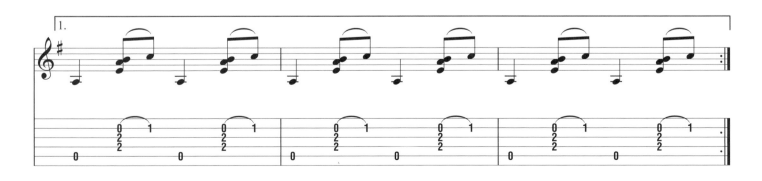

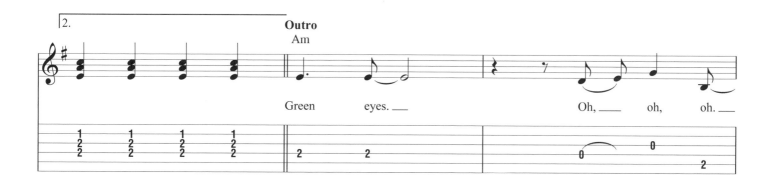

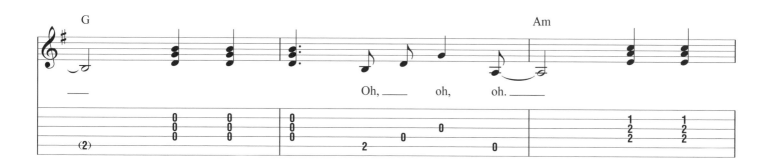

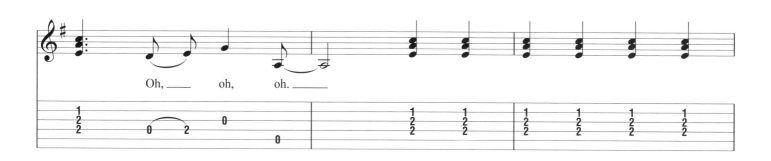

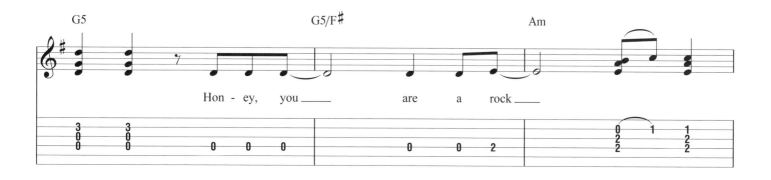

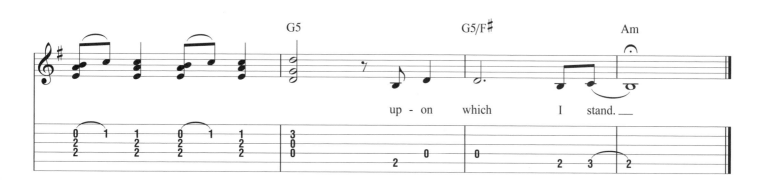

Everglow

Words and Music by Christopher Martin, William Champion, Jonathan Buckland, Guy Berryman, Tor Hermansen and Mikkel Eriksen

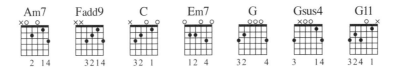

*Capo IV

Strum Pattern: 6
Pick Pattern: 2, 4

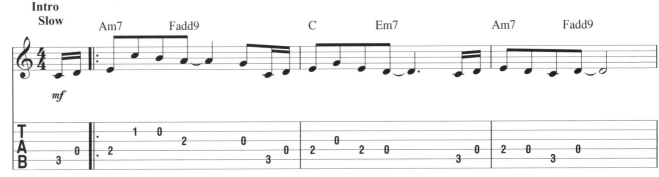

*Optional: To match recording, place capo at 4th fret.

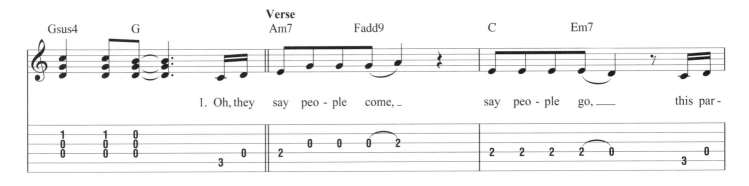

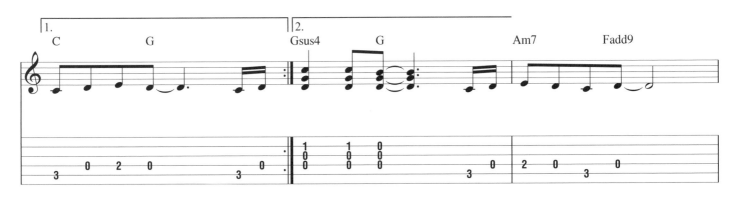

Copyright © 2015 by Universal Music Publishing MGB Ltd. and EMI Music Publishing Ltd.
All Rights for Universal Music Publishing MGB Ltd. in the United States and Canada Administered by Universal Music - MGB Songs
All Rights for EMI Music Publishing Ltd. Administered by Sony/ATV Music Publishing LLC, 424 Church Street, Suite 1200, Nashville, TN 37219
International Copyright Secured   All Rights Reserved

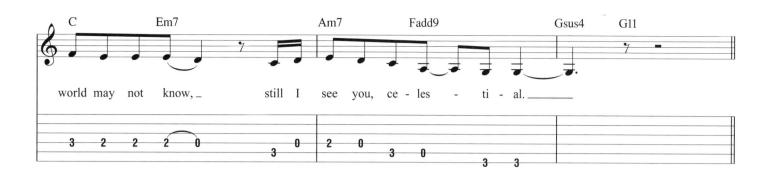

world may not know, _ still I see you, ce - les - ti - al. _____

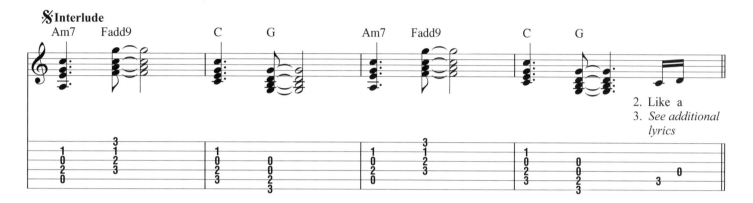

𝄋 Interlude

2. Like a
3. *See additional lyrics*

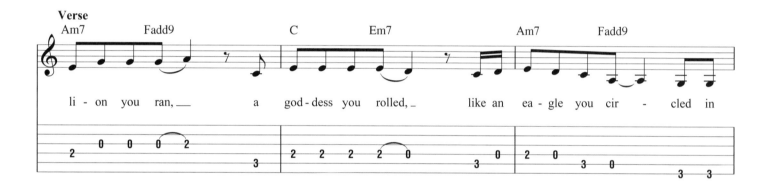

Verse

li - on you ran, _ a god - dess you rolled, _ like an ea - gle you cir - cled in

per - fect pur - ple. _ So how come things move on, __ how come cars don't slow, _ when it

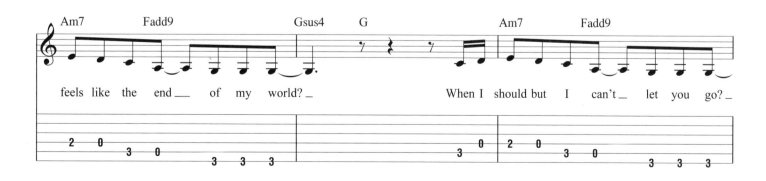

feels like the end __ of my world? _ When I should but I can't _ let you go? _

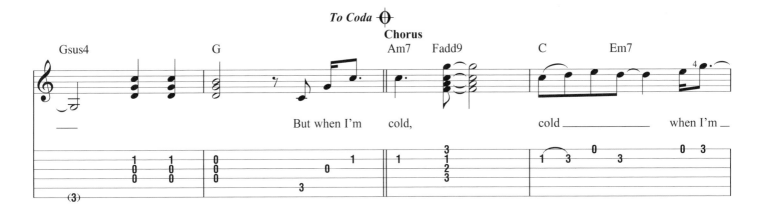

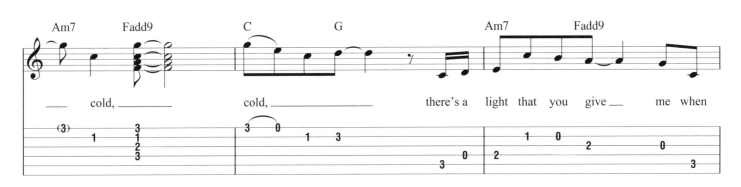

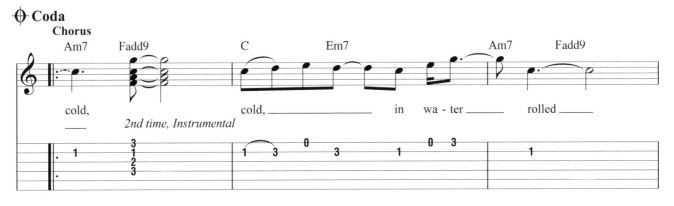

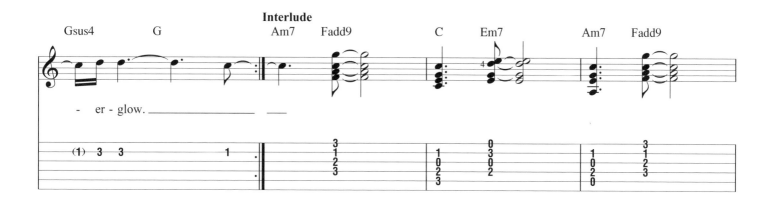

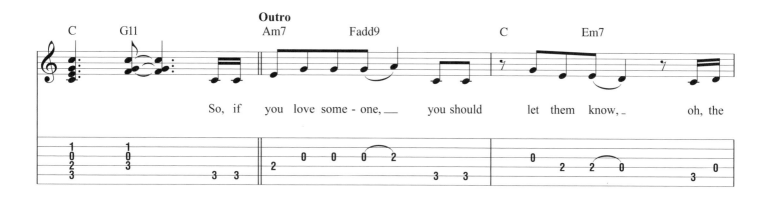

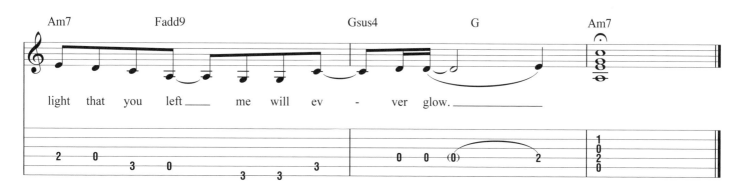

Additional Lyrics

3. Like brothers in blood, sisters who ride,
And we swore on that night we'd be friends till we die.
But the changing of winds and the way waters flow,
Life as short as the falling of snow;
And I'm gonna miss you, I know.

Every Teardrop Is a Waterfall

Words and Music by Guy Berryman, Jon Buckland, Will Champion, Chris Martin, Peter Allen, Adrienne Anderson and Brian Eno

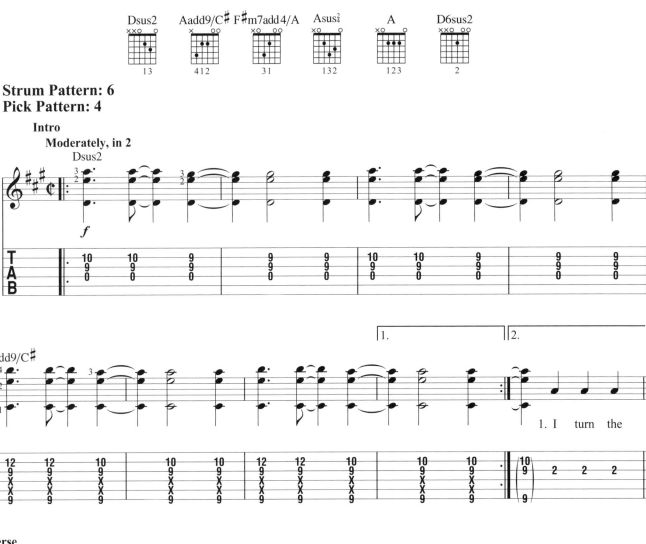

Strum Pattern: 6
Pick Pattern: 4

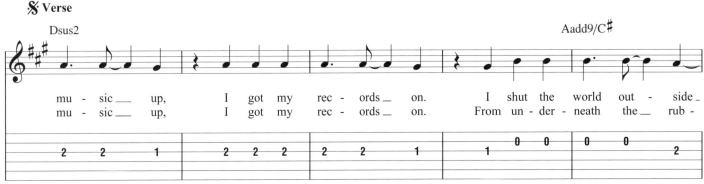

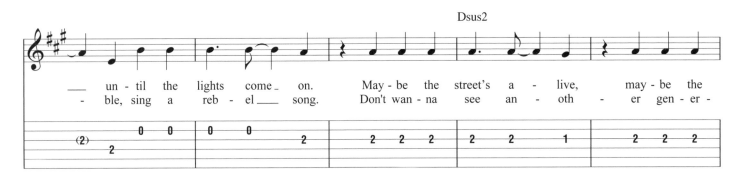

Copyright © 2011 by Universal Music Publishing MGB Ltd., Irving Music, Inc., Woolnough Music, Inc. and Opal Music
All Rights for Universal Music Publishing MGB Ltd. in the United States and Canada Administered by Universal Music - MGB Songs
All Rights for Woolnough Music, Inc. Administered by Irving Music, Inc.
International Copyright Secured   All Rights Reserved

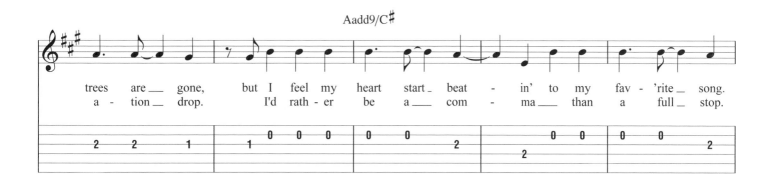

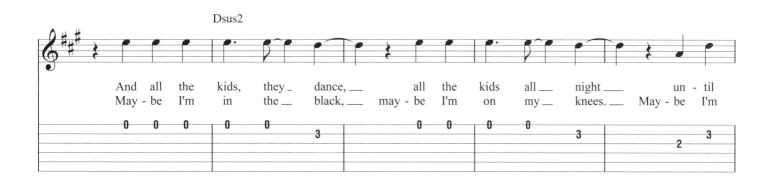

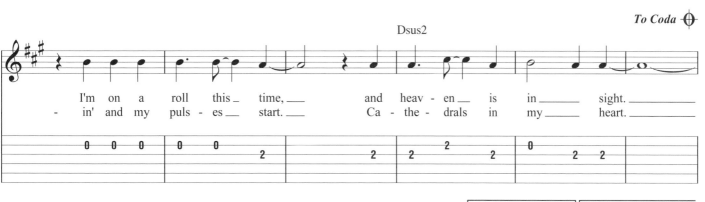

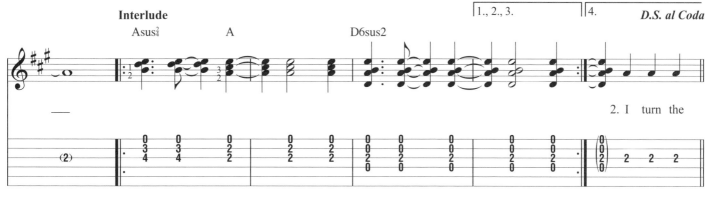

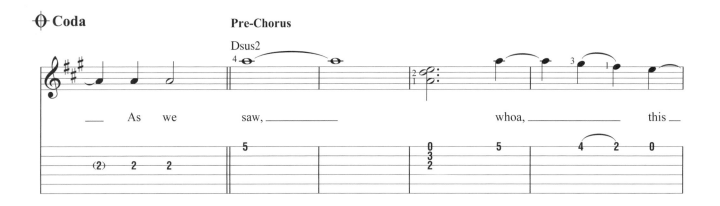

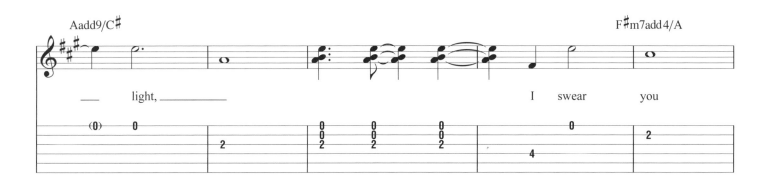

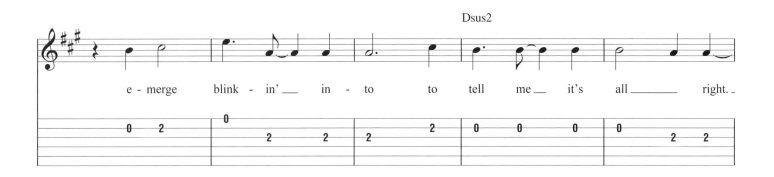

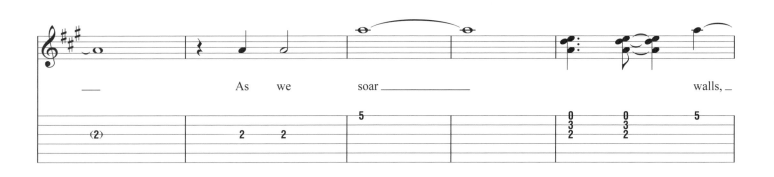

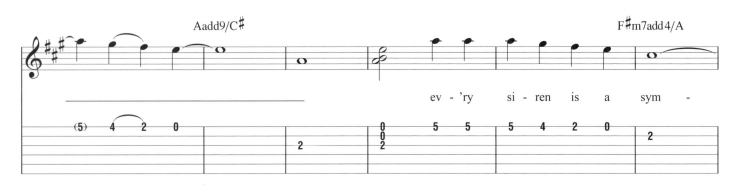

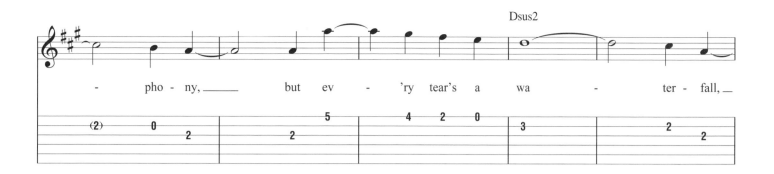

-pho - ny, _____ but ev - 'ry tear's a wa - ter - fall, _____

Chorus

_____ is a wa - ter - fall, _____ ah, _____ is a wa - ter - fall, _

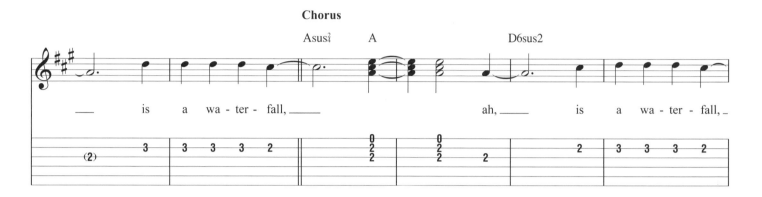

_____ ah, _____ is a wa - ter - fall. _____

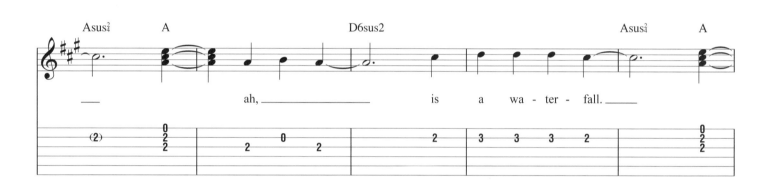

Ev - 'ry tear - drop is a wa - ter - fall, _____ ah. _____

Bridge

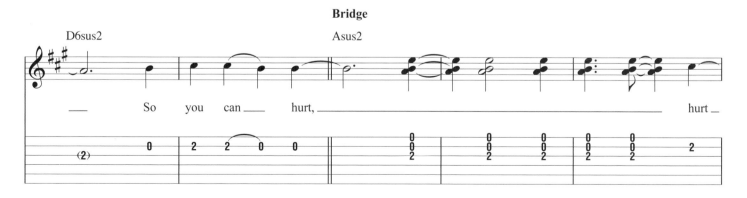

_____ So you can _____ hurt, _____ hurt _

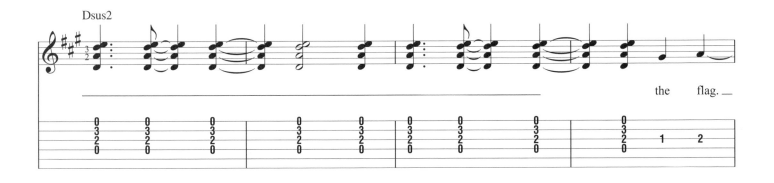

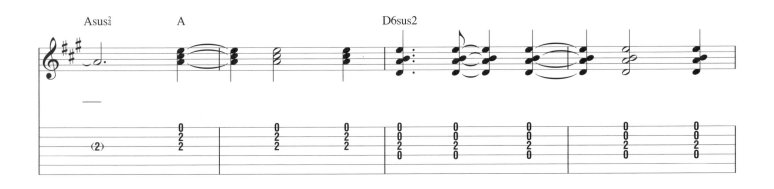

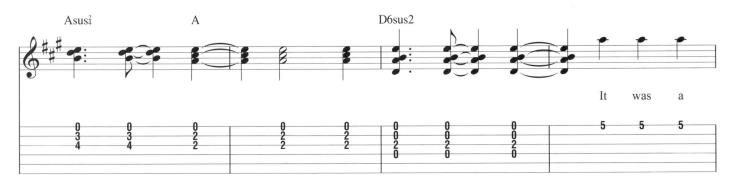

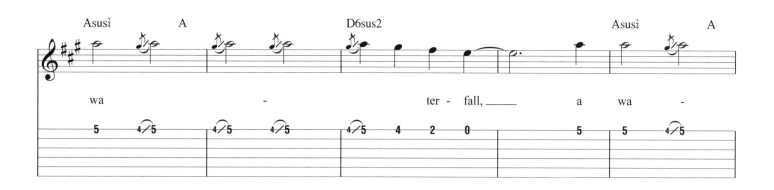

wa - - ter - fall, ____ a wa -

- ter - fall. ____

Outro

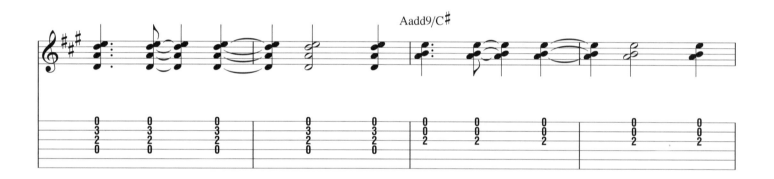

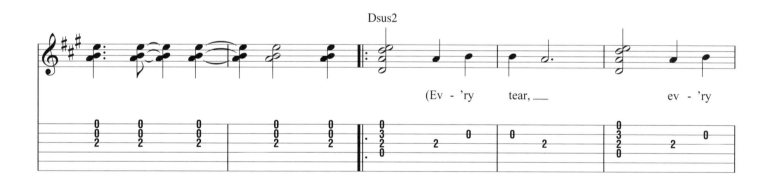

(Ev - 'ry tear, ___ ev - 'ry

Repeat and fade

tear, ___ ev - 'ry tear - drop is a wa - ter - fall.)

Fix You

Words and Music by Guy Berryman, Jon Buckland, Will Champion and Chris Martin

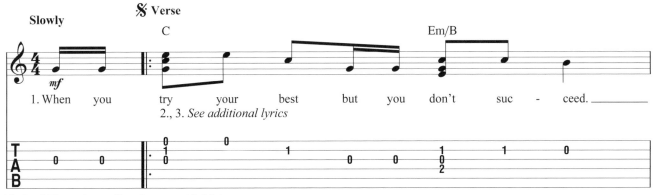

*Capo III

Strum Pattern: 1
Pick Pattern: 5

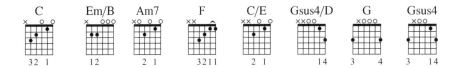

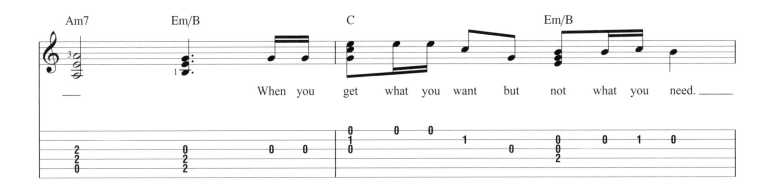

*Optional: To match recording, place capo at 3rd fret.

Copyright © 2005 by Universal Music Publishing MGB Ltd.
All Rights in the United States Administered by Universal Music - MGB Songs
International Copyright Secured   All Rights Reserved

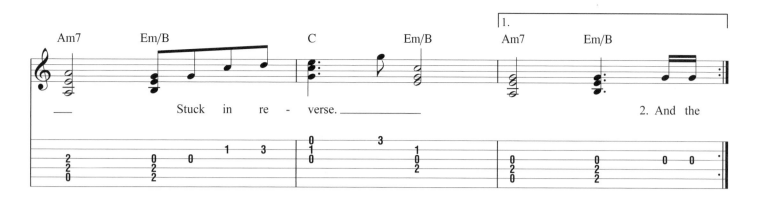

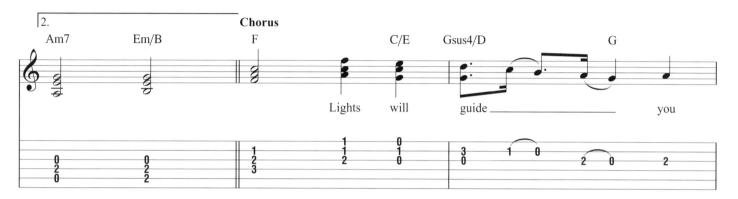

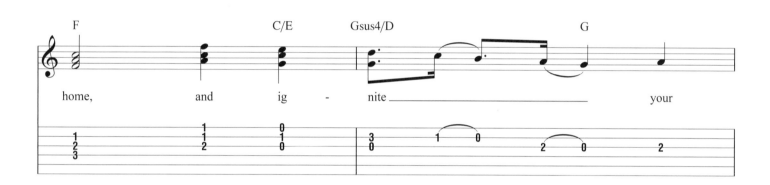

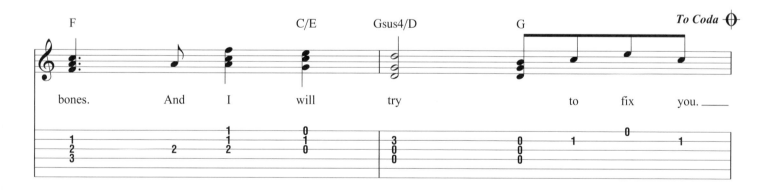

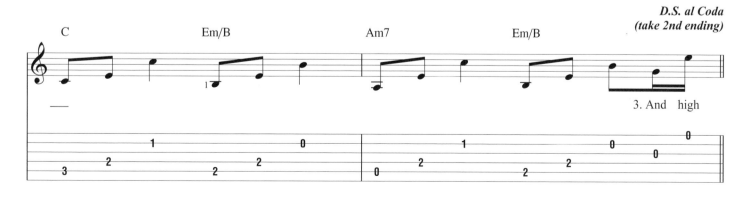

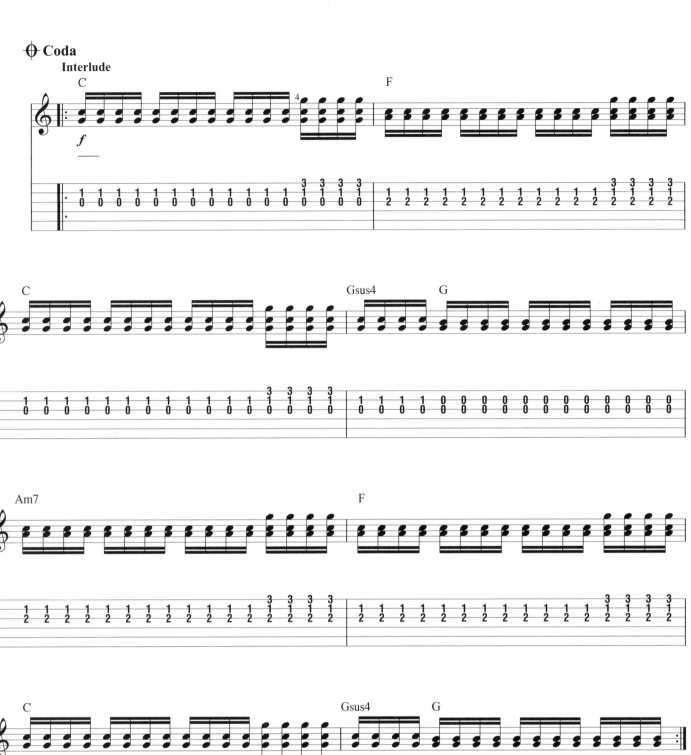

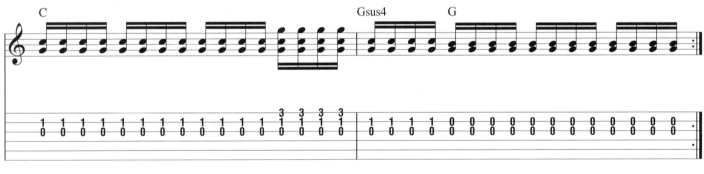

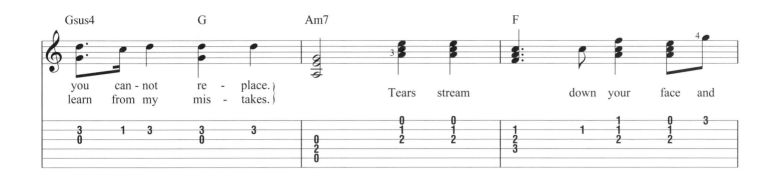

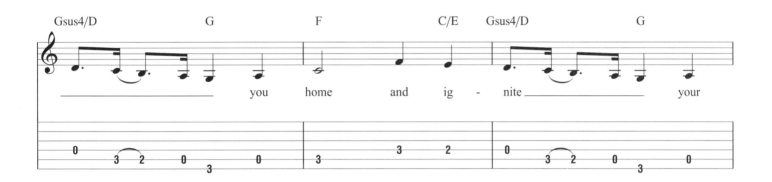

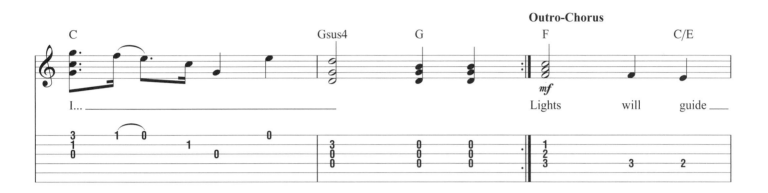

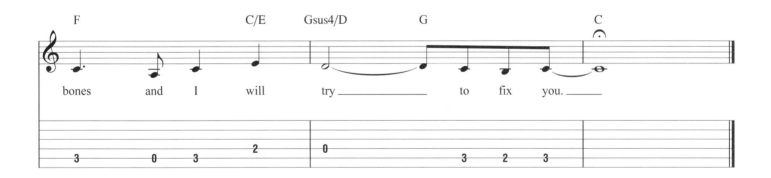

Additional Lyrics

2. And the tears come streaming down your face
When you lose something you can't replace.
When you love someone but it goes to waste
Could it be worse?

3. And high up above or down below
When you're too in love to let it go.
But if you never try you'll never know
Just what you're worth.

Hymn for the Weekend

Words and Music by Christopher Martin, William Champion, Jonathan Buckland, Guy Berryman,
Tor Hermansen, Mikkel Eriksen, Marcos Tovar, Venor Yard and Scott Zant

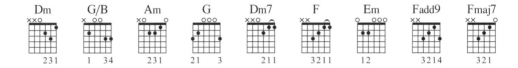

*Capo III

Strum Pattern: 1
Pick Pattern: 2, 5

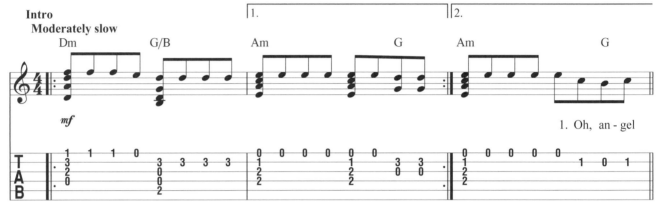

*Optional: To match recording place capo at 3rd fret.

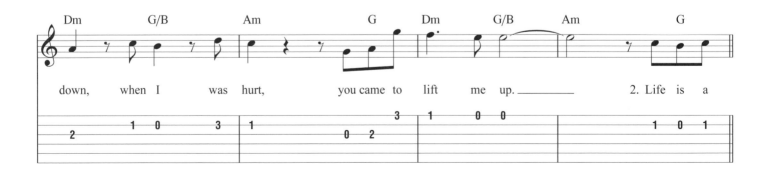

Copyright © 2015 by Universal Music Publishing MGB Ltd., EMI Music Publishing Ltd. and Reach Global UK (Ltd.)
All Rights for Universal Music Publishing MGB Ltd. in the United States and Canada Administered by Universal Music - MGB Songs
All Rights for EMI Music Publishing Ltd. Administered by Sony/ATV Music Publishing LLC, 424 Church Street, Suite 1200, Nashville, TN 37219
International Copyright Secured   All Rights Reserved

Verse

drink and love's a drug. Oh, now I think I must be miles ____
sent from up a - bove, I feel you cours - ing through my

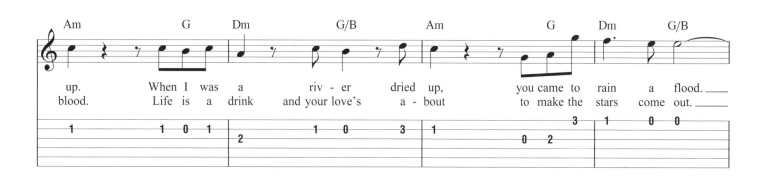

up. When I was a riv - er dried up, you came to rain a flood. ____
blood. Life is a drink and your love's a - bout to make the stars come out. ____

Pre-Chorus

____ You said, "Drink from me, drink from me" when I was so thirst - y. Pour on a
____ (3.) Put your wings on me, wings on me when I was so heav - y. Pour on a

sym - pho - ny; now I just can't get e - nough. ____ Put your wings on low, ____ low, ____ low, ____ low. ____
sym - pho - ny; when I'm

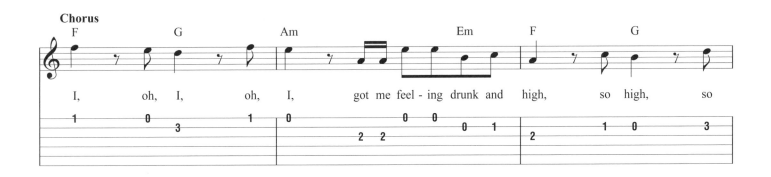

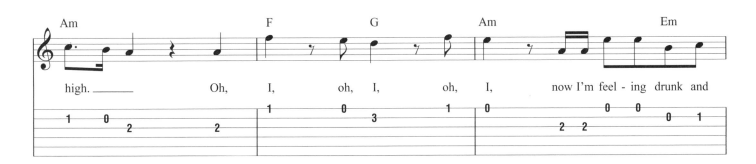

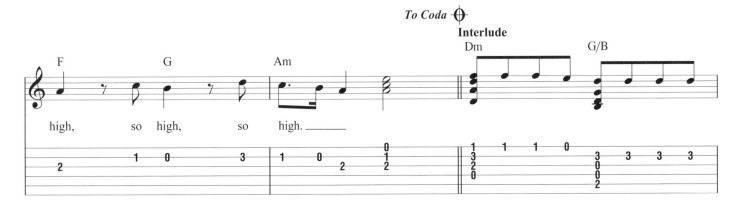

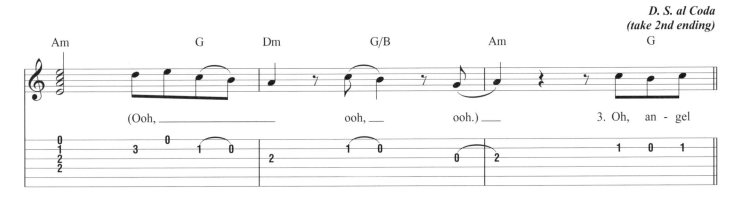

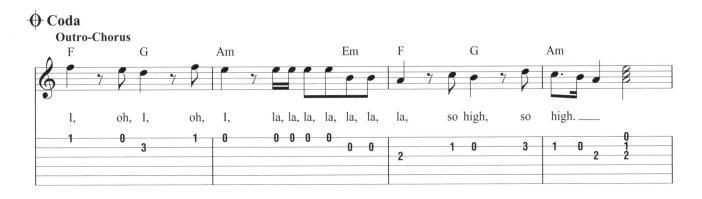

I, oh, I, oh, I, now I'm feel-ing drunk and high, so high, so

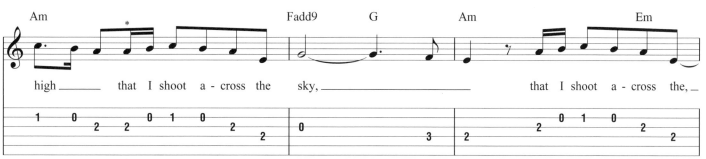

high _____ that I shoot a-cross the sky, _____ that I shoot a-cross the, _____

*Sung one octave higher to end.

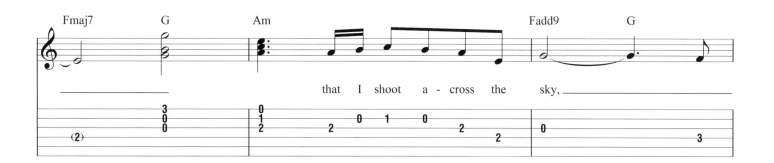

_____ that I shoot a-cross the sky, _____

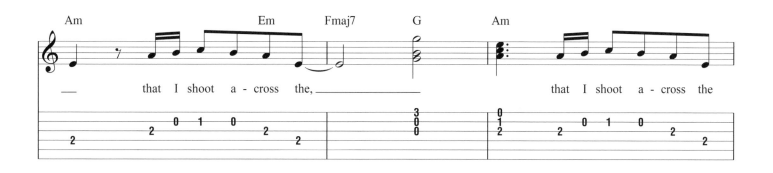

_____ that I shoot a-cross the, _____ that I shoot a-cross the

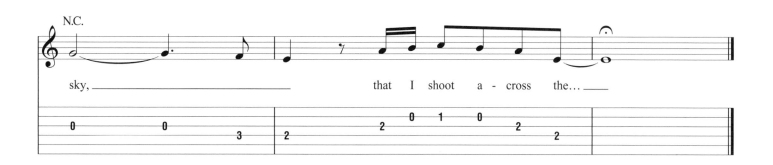

sky, _____ that I shoot a-cross the... _____

In My Place

Words and Music by Guy Berryman, Jon Buckland, Will Champion and Chris Martin

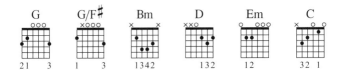

*Capo II

Strum Pattern: 1
Pick Pattern: 5

Intro
Slowly

*Optional: To match recording, place capo at 2nd fret.

Verse

1. In my place, in my place were lines that I could-n't
2. *See additional lyrics*

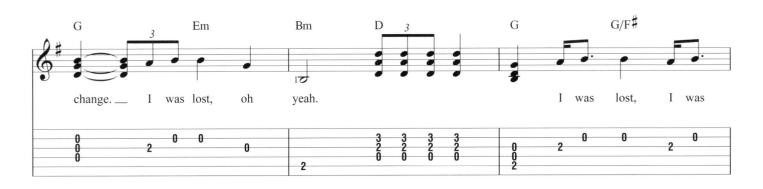

change.__ I was lost, oh yeah. I was lost, I was

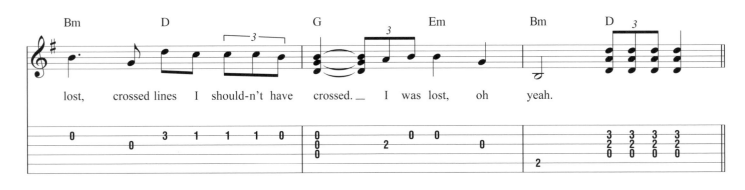

lost, crossed lines I should-n't have crossed.__ I was lost, oh yeah.

Copyright © 2002 by Universal Music Publishing MGB Ltd.
All Rights in the United States Administered by Universal Music - MGB Songs
International Copyright Secured   All Rights Reserved

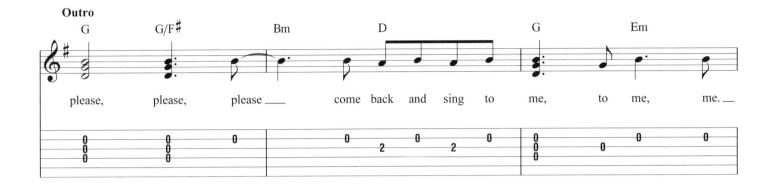

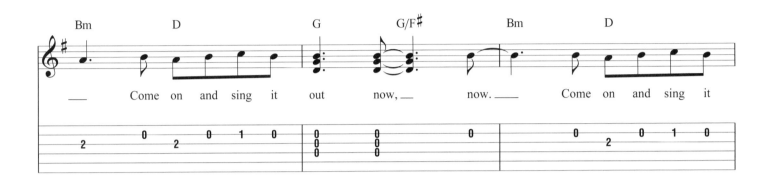

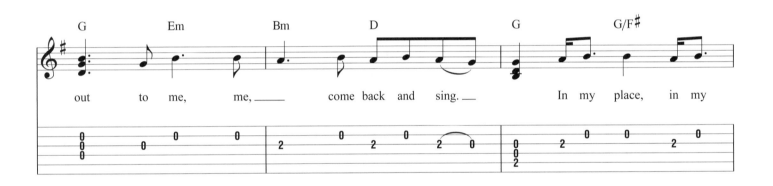

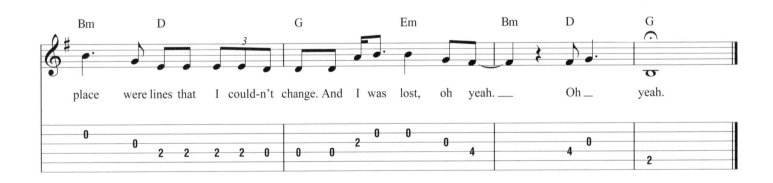

Additional Lyrics

2. I was scared, I was scared,
   Tired and under-prepared
   But I'll wait for it.
   And if you go, if you go
   And leave me down here on my own,
   Then I'll wait for you, yeah.

Lost!

Words and Music by Guy Berryman, Jon Buckland, Will Champion and Chris Martin

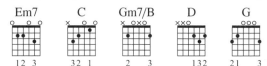

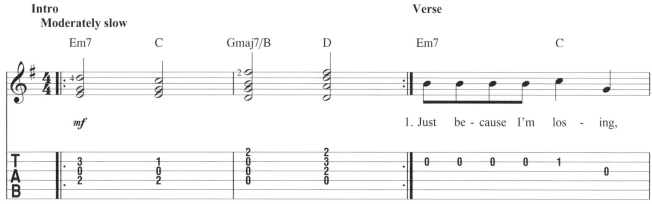

*Strum Pattern: 1
*Pick Pattern: 5

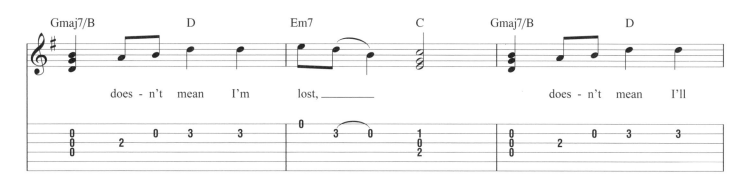

*Use Pattern 10 for 2/4 meas.

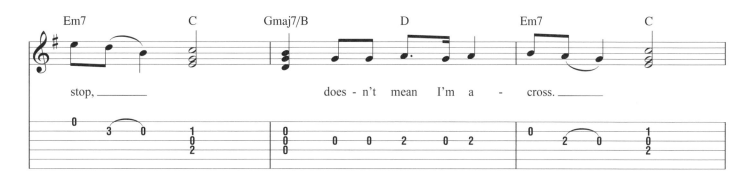

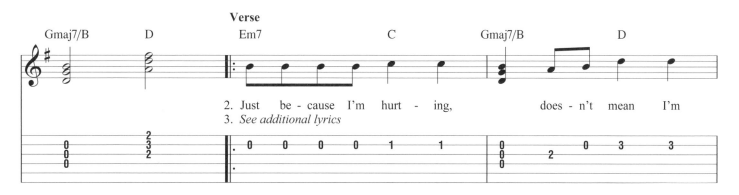

Copyright © 2008 by Universal Music Publishing MGB Ltd.
All Rights in the United States and Canada Administered by Universal Music - MGB Songs
International Copyright Secured   All Rights Reserved

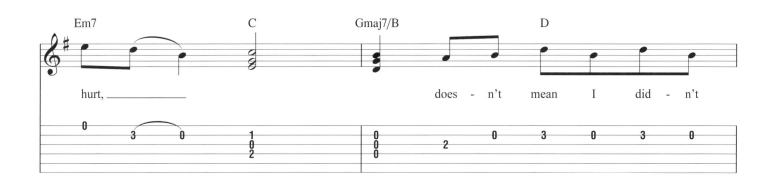

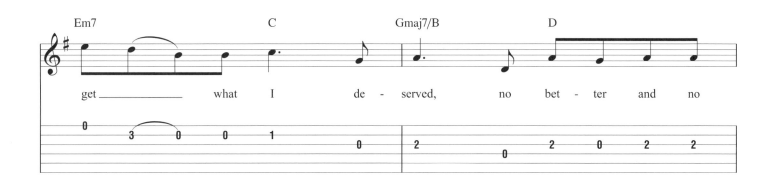

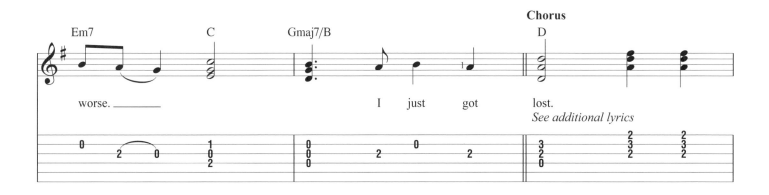

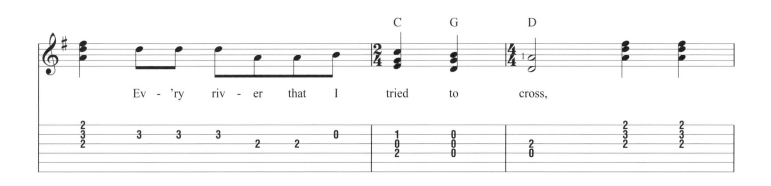

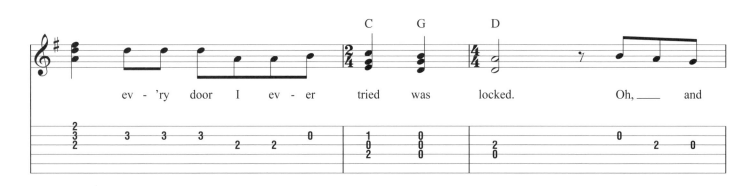

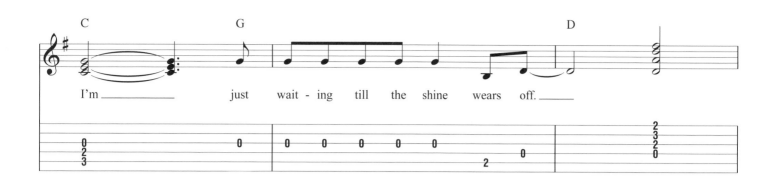

I'm _____ just wait - ing till the shine wears off. _____

1. **2.** **Outro**

Oh, _____ and I'm _____ just

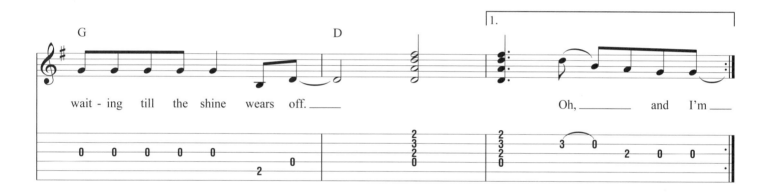

wait - ing till the shine wears off. _____ **1.** Oh, _____ and I'm _____

2. ***Repeat and fade***

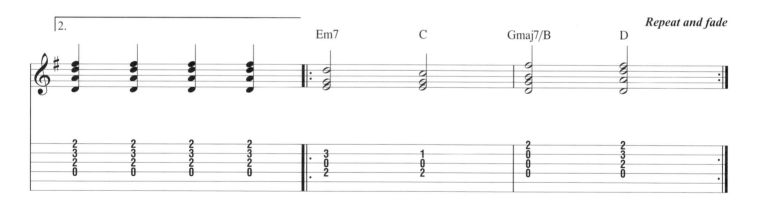

Additional Lyrics

3. You might be a big fish in a little pond,
   Doesn't mean you've won, 'cause along may come
   A bigger one.

Chorus And you'll be lost.
   Ev'ry river that you tried to cross,
   Ev'ry gun you ever held went off.
   Oh, and I'm just waiting till the firing's stopped.

Magic

Words and Music by Guy Berryman, Jon Buckland, Will Champion and Chris Martin

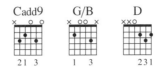

*Capo II

Strum Pattern: 3, 4
Pick Pattern: 3, 4

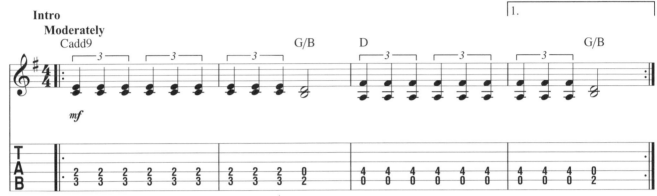

*Optional: To match recording, place capo at 2nd fret.

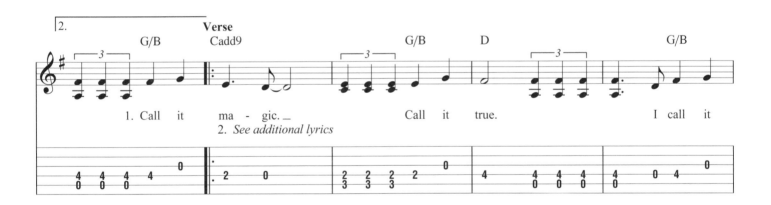

1. Call it ma - gic. _ Call it true. I call it
2. *See additional lyrics*

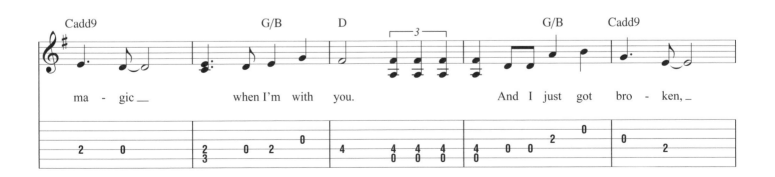

ma - gic _ when I'm with you. And I just got bro - ken, _

Copyright © 2014 by Universal Music Publishing MGB Ltd.
All Rights in the United States and Canada Administered by Universal Music - MGB Songs
International Copyright Secured   All Rights Reserved

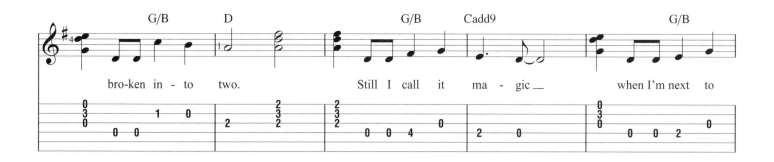

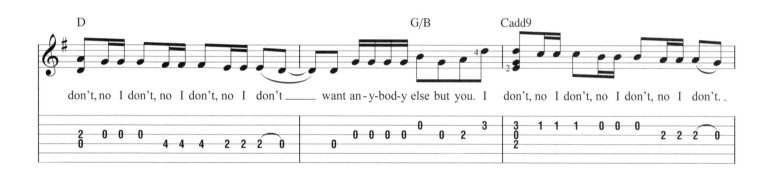

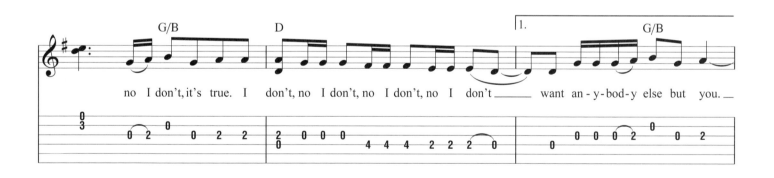

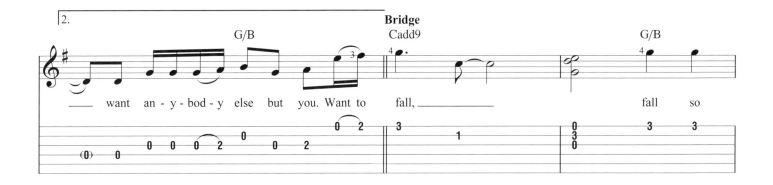

want an-y-bod-y else but you. Want to fall, _____ fall so

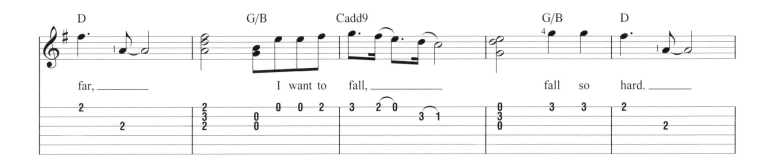

far, _____ I want to fall, _____ fall so hard. _____

And I call it ma - gic. _ And I call it true. I call it

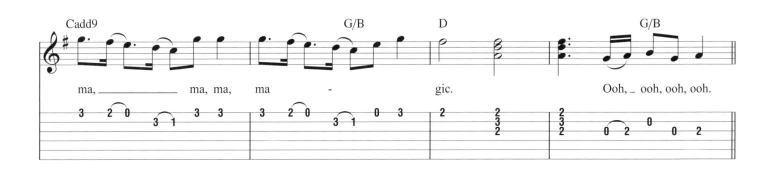

ma, _____ ma, ma, ma - gic. Ooh, _ ooh, ooh, ooh.

Interlude

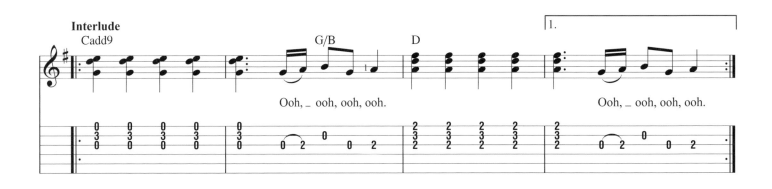

Ooh, _ ooh, ooh, ooh. Ooh, _ ooh, ooh, ooh.

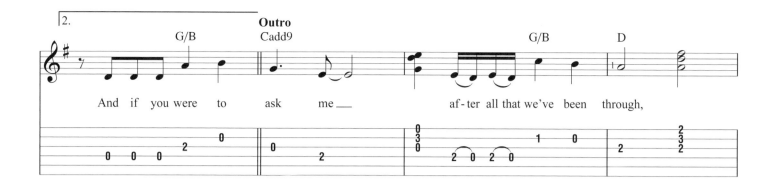

And if you were to ask me ___ af-ter all that we've been through,

"Still be-lieve in ma - gic?" Well, yes I do. Yes, I

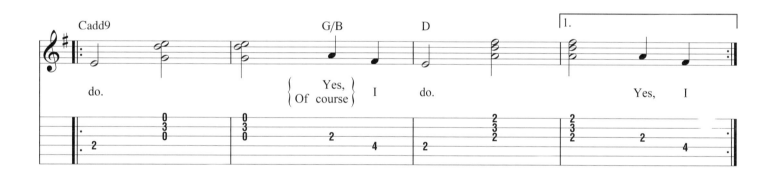

do. Yes, Of course I do. Yes, I

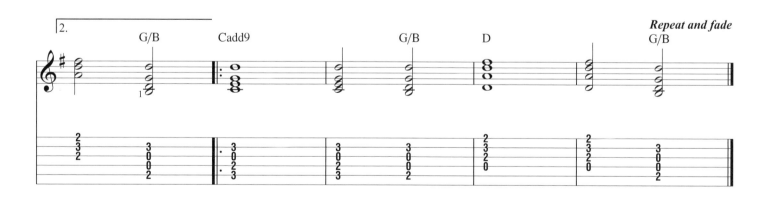

Additional Lyrics

2. Call it magic. Cut me into two.
And with all your magic I disappear from view.
And I can't get over, can't get over you.
Still I call it magic, you're such a precious jewel.

Paradise

Words and Music by Guy Berryman, Jon Buckland, Will Champion, Chris Martin and Brian Eno

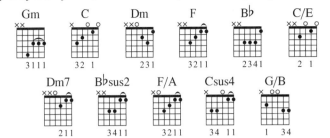

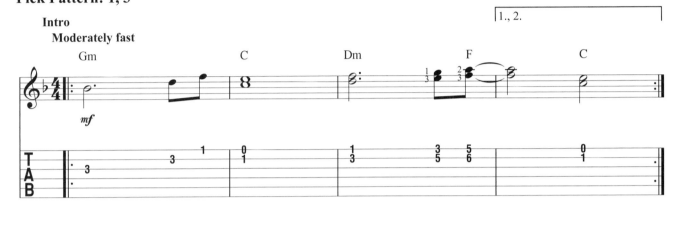

Strum Pattern: 3, 4
Pick Pattern: 1, 3

Intro
Moderately fast

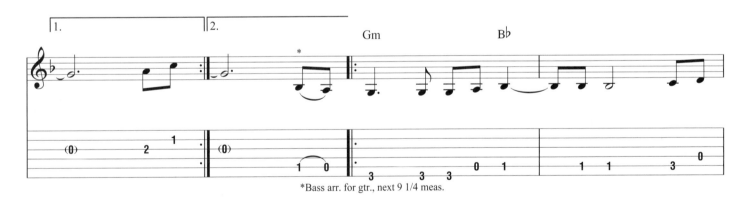

*Bass arr. for gtr., next 9 1/4 meas.

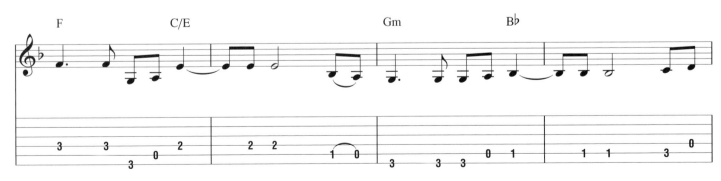

Copyright © 2011 by Universal Music Publishing MGB Ltd. and Opal Ltd.
All Rights for Universal Music Publishing MGB Ltd. in the United States and Canada Administered by Universal Music - MGB Songs
International Copyright Secured   All Rights Reserved

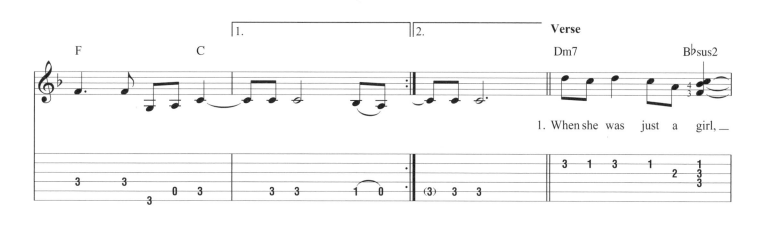

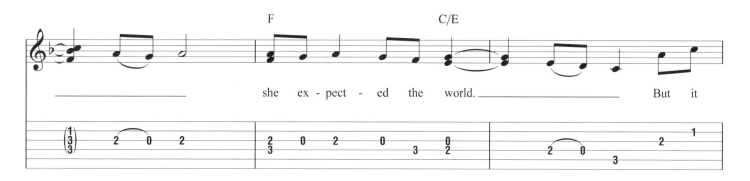

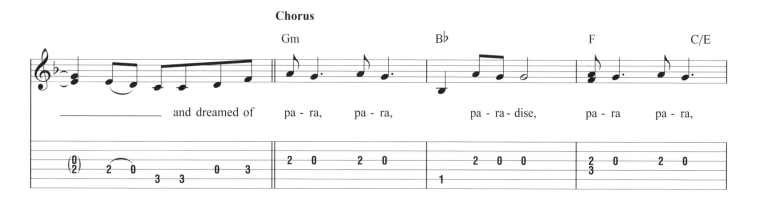

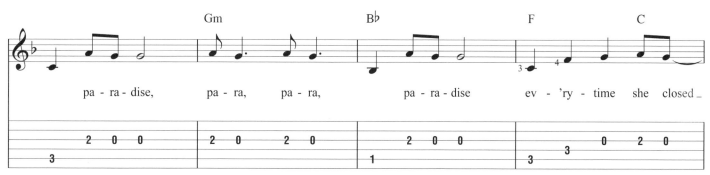

Interlude

her eyes. * Oo,   oo.

*Lyrics sung 2nd time.

Verse

2. When she was   just   a   girl,

she ex - pect - ed the world.   But it flew a - way from her reach

and the bul - lets catch in her teeth.

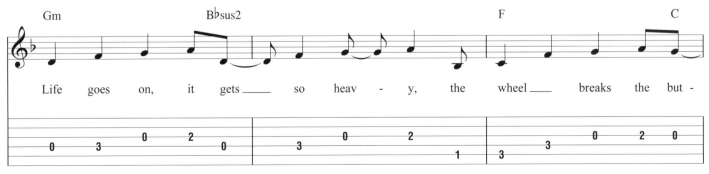

Life   goes   on,   it   gets   so   heav - y,   the   wheel   breaks   the   but -

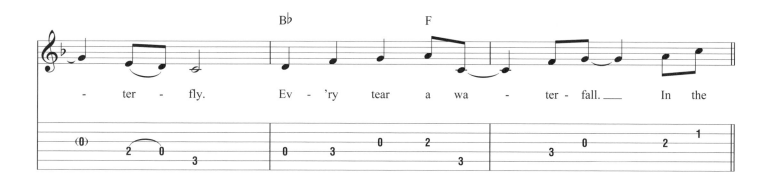

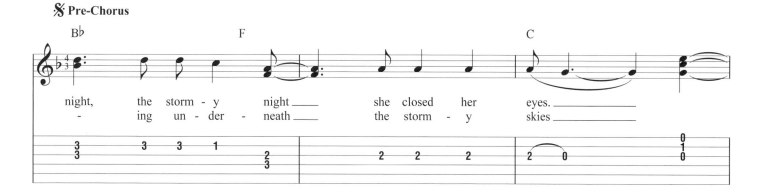

Pre-Chorus

Chorus

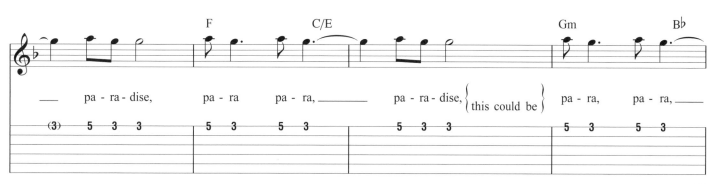

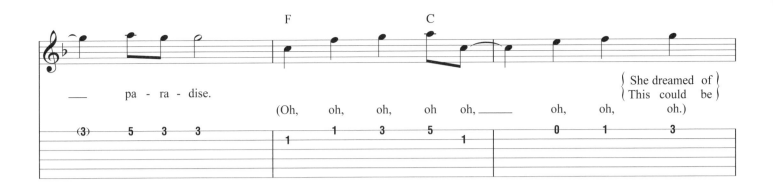

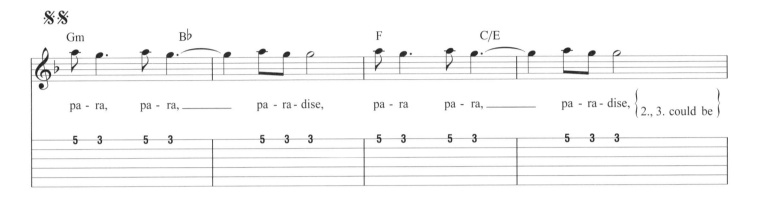

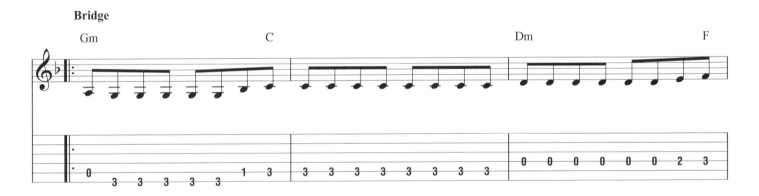

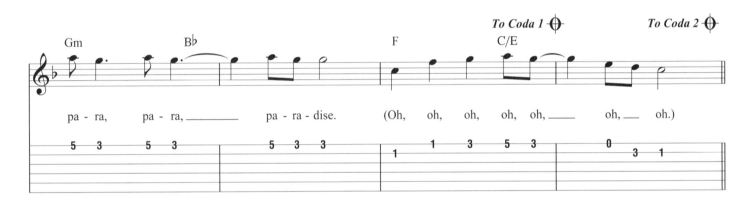

The Scientist

Words and Music by Guy Berryman, Jon Buckland, Will Champion and Chris Martin

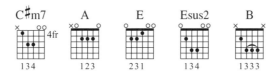

*Capo 1

Strum Pattern: 1
Pick Pattern: 3

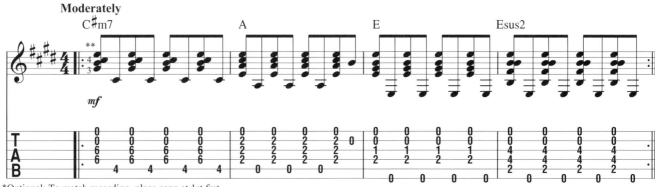

*Optional: To match recording, place capo at 1st fret.
**Piano arr. for gtr., next 4 meas.

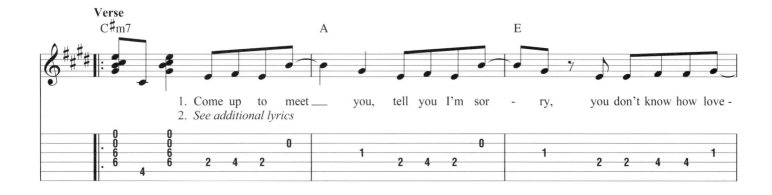

1. Come up to meet___ you, tell you I'm sor - ry, you don't know how love -
2. *See additional lyrics*

- ly you are. ___ I had to find___ you, tell you I need___ you, tell you I'll set___

Copyright © 2002 by Universal Music Publishing MGB Ltd.
All Rights in the United States Administered by Universal Music - MGB Songs
International Copyright Secured   All Rights Reserved

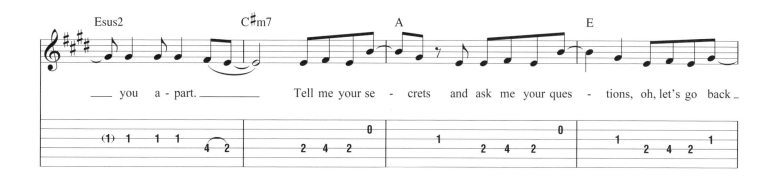

you a - part. Tell me your se - crets and ask me your ques - tions, oh, let's go back

to the start. Run - ning in cir - cles, com - ing in tails, heads are a sci-

Chorus

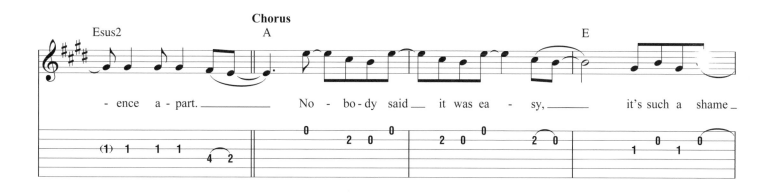

- ence a - part. No - bo - dy said it was ea - sy, it's such a shame

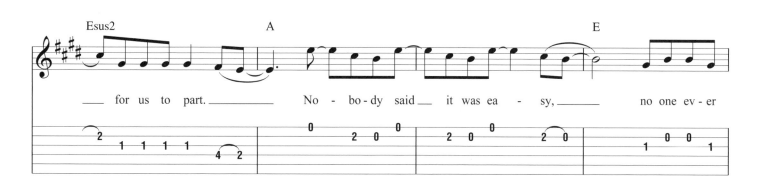

for us to part. No - bo - dy said it was ea - sy, no one ev - er

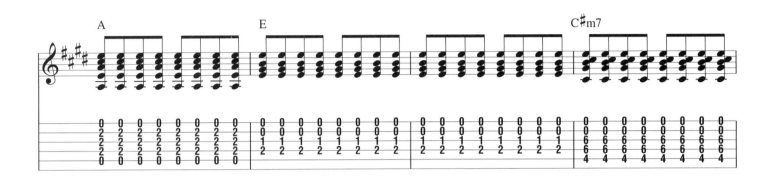

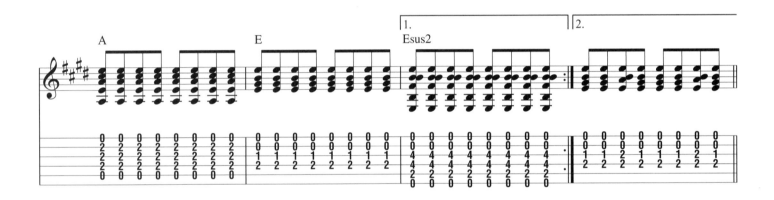

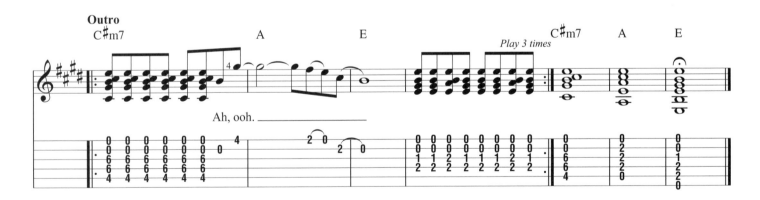

Additional Lyrics

2. I was just guessing at numbers and figures,
   Pulling the puzzles apart.
   Questions of science, science and progress
   Do not speak as loud as my heart.
   And tell me you love me and come back and haunt me,
   Oh, when I rush to the start.
   Running in circles, chasing our tails,
   Coming a back as we are.

A Sky Full of Stars

Words and Music by Guy Berryman, Jon Buckland, Will Champion, Chris Martin and Tim Bergling

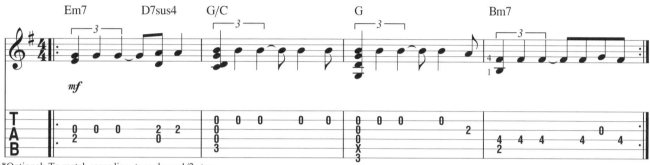

*Tune down 1/2 step:
(low to high) Eb-Ab-Db-Gb-Bb-Eb

Strum Pattern: 6
Pick Pattern: 1

*Optional: To match recording, tune down 1/2 step.

Copyright © 2014 by Universal Music Publishing MGB Ltd. and EMI Blackwood Music Inc.
All Rights for Universal Music Publishing MGB Ltd. in the United States and Canada Administered by Universal Music - MGB Songs
All Rights for EMI Blackwood Music Inc. Administered by Sony/ATV Music Publishing LLC, 424 Church Street, Suite 1200, Nashville, TN 37219
International Copyright Secured   All Rights Reserved

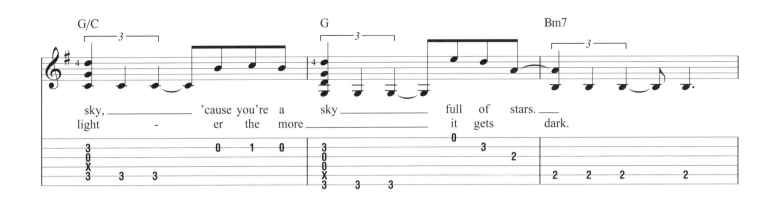

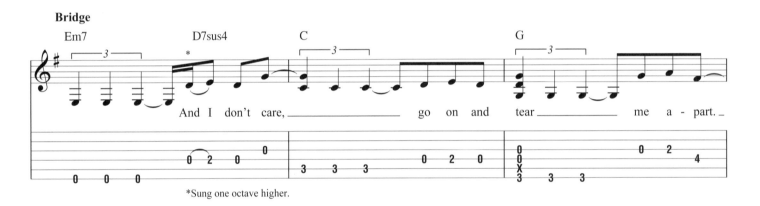

*Sung one octave higher.

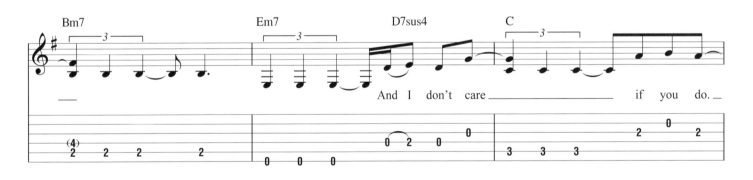

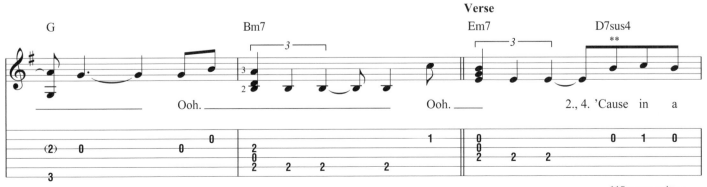

**Sung as written.

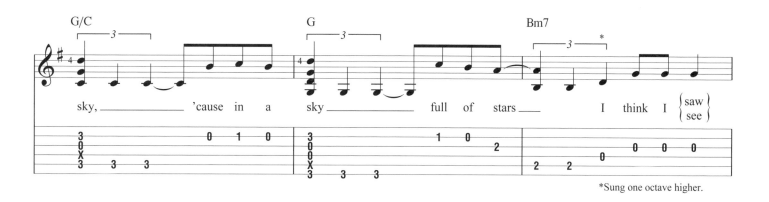

sky, _____ 'cause in a sky _____ full of stars ___ I think I { saw / see }

*Sung one octave higher.

To Coda ⊕

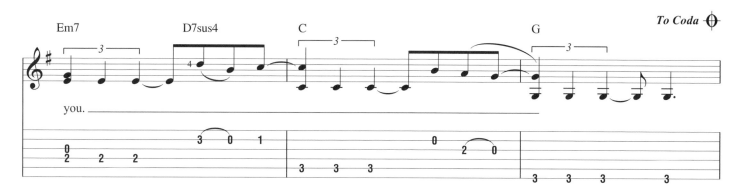

you.

Interlude

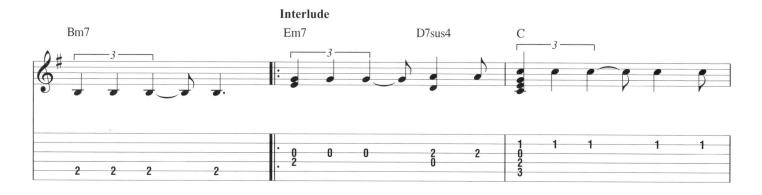

1., 2.   3.   *D.S. al Coda*

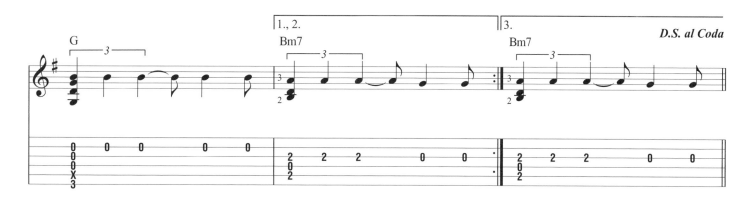

⊕ **Coda**

I think I see you. _____

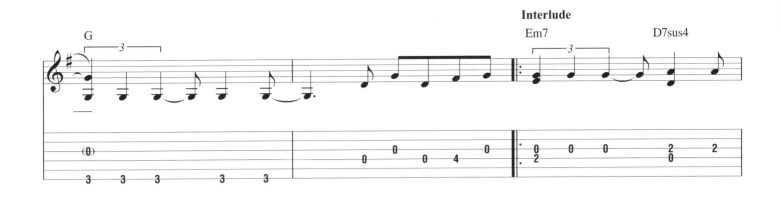

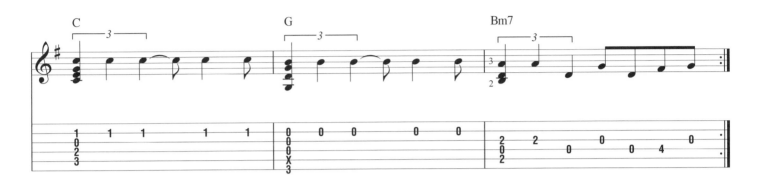

Verse

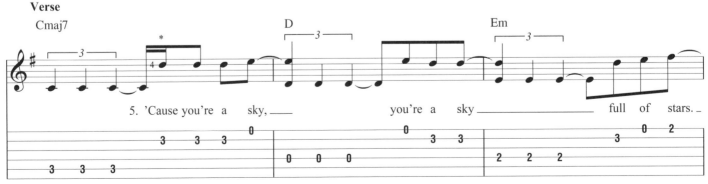

5. 'Cause you're a sky, ____ you're a sky _____ full of stars. ___

*Sung as written.

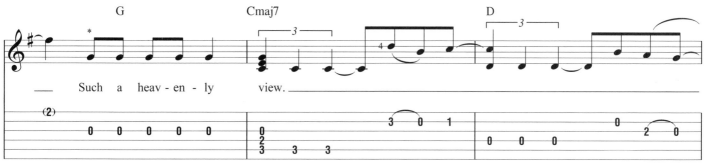

Such a heav - en - ly view. _____

*Sung one octave higher.

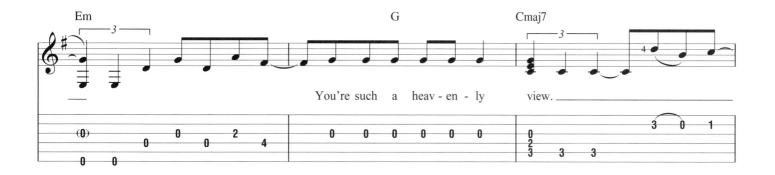

You're such a heav - en - ly view. _____

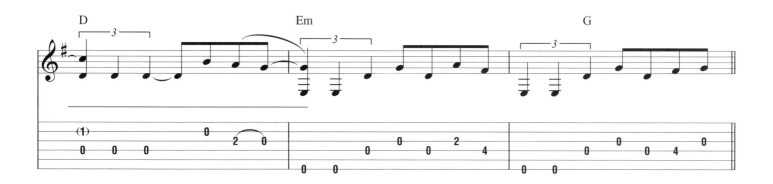

Outro

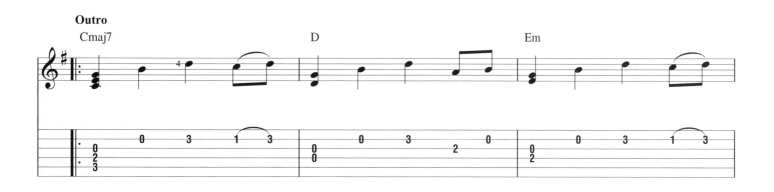

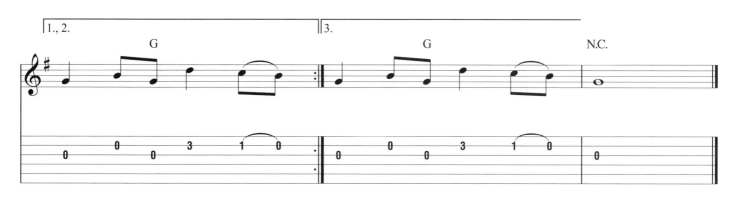

Shiver

Words and Music by Guy Berryman, Jon Buckland, Will Champion and Chris Martin

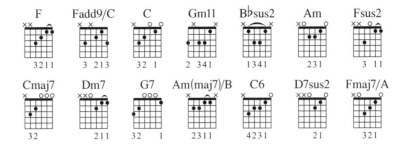

*Tune down 1/2 step:

(low to high) Eb-Ab-Db-Gb-Bb-Eb

Strum Pattern: 8

Pick Pattern: 8

Intro

  Moderately, in 2

*Optional: To match recording, tune down 1/2 step.

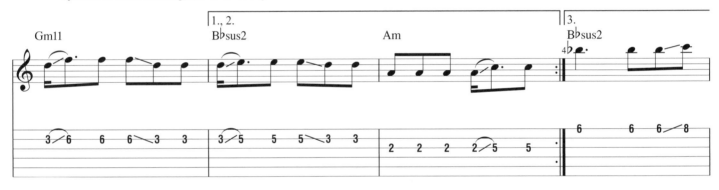

Verse

1. So I look in your di-rec-tion,_ but you

2. *See additional lyrics*

pay me no at-ten-tion,_ do you? _____

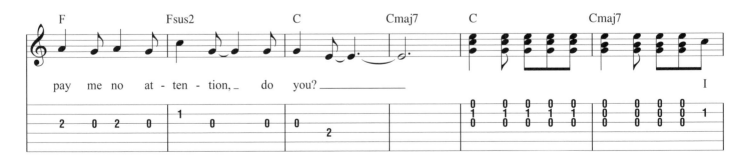

Copyright © 2000 by Universal Music Publishing MGB Ltd.

All Rights in the United States Administered by Universal Music - MGB Songs

International Copyright Secured All Rights Reserved

know you don't lis - ten to me 'cause you say you see straight through me, don't you? _____

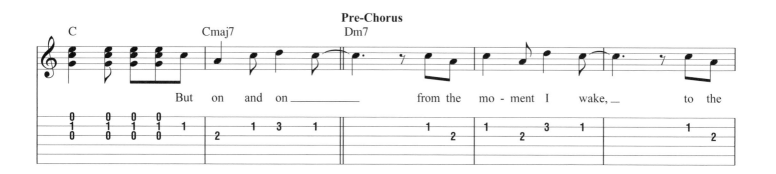

But on and on _____ from the mo - ment I wake, _ to the

Pre-Chorus

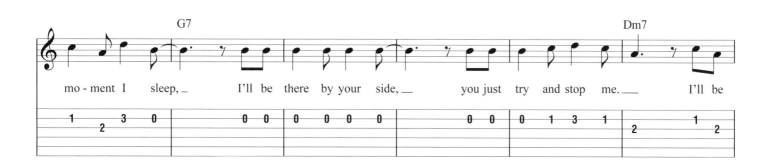

mo - ment I sleep, _ I'll be there by your side, _ you just try and stop me. _ I'll be

wait - ing in line _ just to see if you _ care. _____ Oh. _____

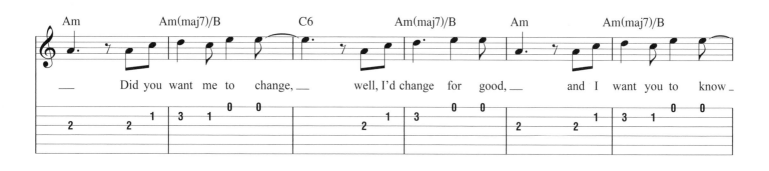

_ Did you want me to change, _ well, I'd change for good, _ and I want you to know _

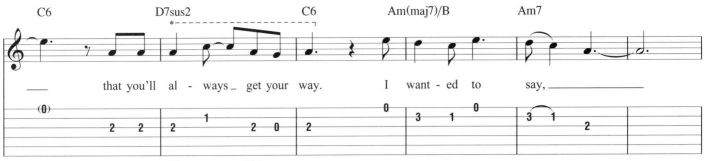

*Sung one octave higher.

Chorus

**Sung one octave higher, next 13 meas.

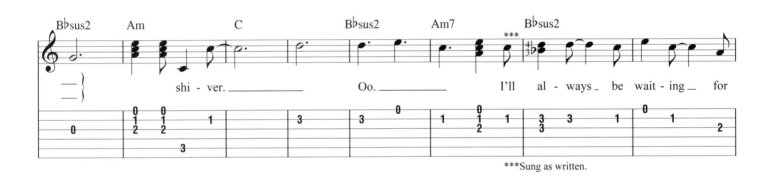

***Sung as written.

Interlude

Bridge

waiting. And it's you I see but you don't see me. And it's you I hear, so

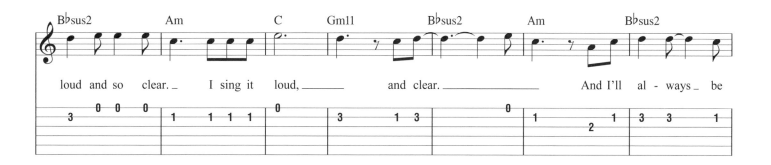

loud and so clear. I sing it loud, and clear. And I'll always be

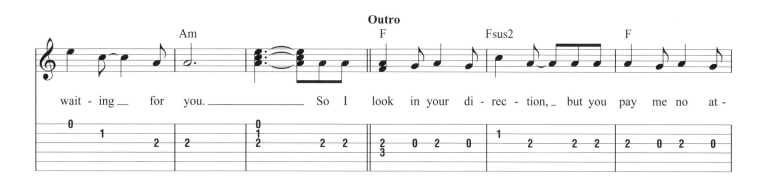

Outro

waiting for you. So I look in your direction, but you pay me no at-

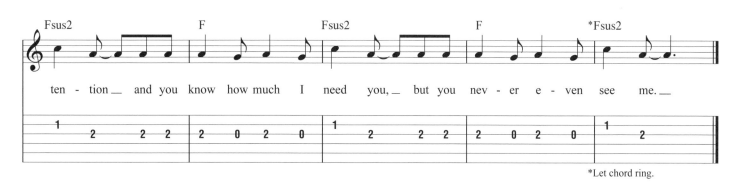

tention and you know how much I need you, but you never even see me.

*Let chord ring.

Additional Lyrics

2. So you know how much I need you,
But you never even see me, do you?
And is this my final chance of getting you?

Trouble

Words and Music by Guy Berryman, Jon Buckland, Will Champion and Chris Martin

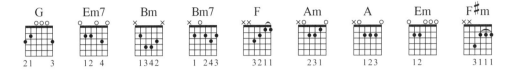

Strum Pattern: 1
Pick Pattern: 1

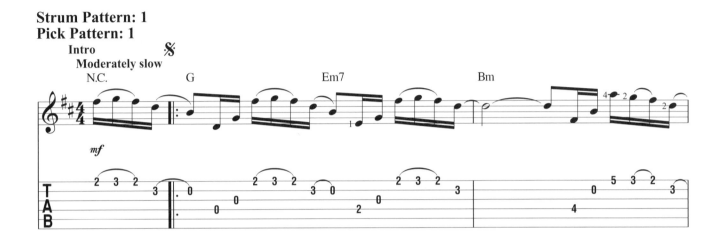

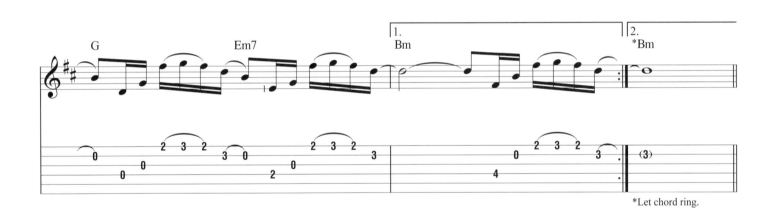

*Let chord ring.

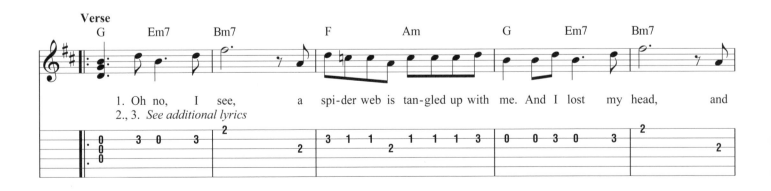

1. Oh no,   I   see,   a   spi-der web   is tan-gled up   with me. And I lost   my head,   and
2., 3. *See additional lyrics*

Copyright © 2000 by Universal Music Publishing MGB Ltd.
All Rights in the United States Administered by Universal Music - MGB Songs
International Copyright Secured   All Rights Reserved

*Let chord ring.

**Let chord ring.

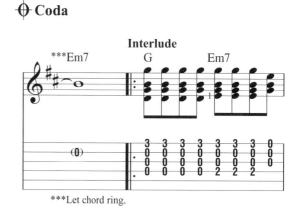

***Let chord ring.

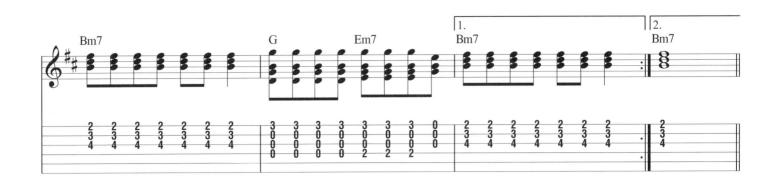

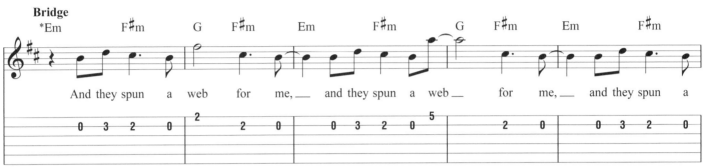

*Let chords ring throughout Bridge.

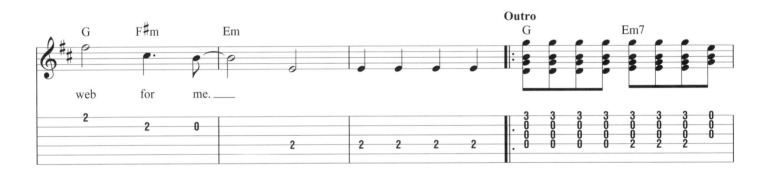

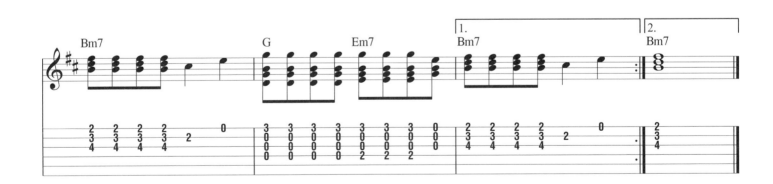

Additional Lyrics

2. Oh no, what's this?
   A spider web and I'm caught in the middle.
   So I turn to run,
   And I thought of all the stupid things I'd done.

3. Oh no, I see,
   A spider web and it's me in the middle.
   So I twist and turn,
   But here am I in my little bubble.
   Singing out ah…

Violet Hill

Words and Music by Guy Berryman, Jon Buckland, Will Champion and Chris Martin

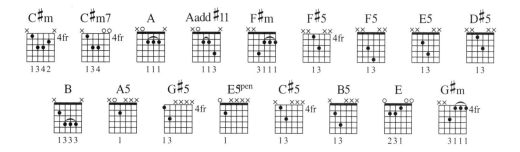

Strum Pattern: 4
Pick Pattern: 1

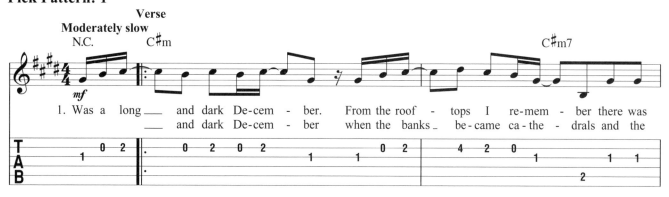

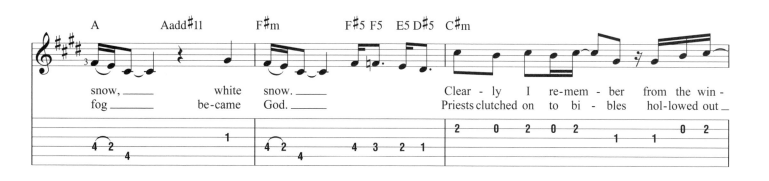

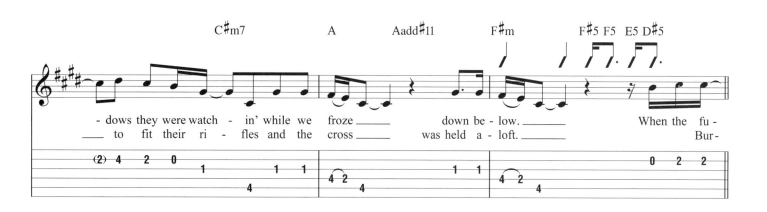

Copyright © 2000 by Universal Music Publishing MGB Ltd.
All Rights in the United States and Canada Administered by Universal Music - MGB Songs
International Copyright Secured   All Rights Reserved

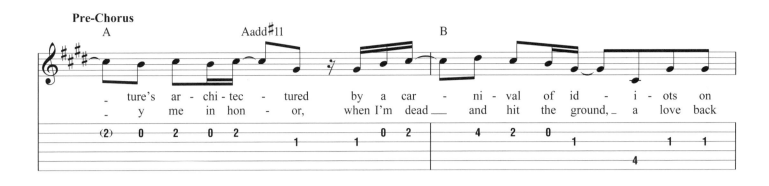

Pre-Chorus

__ture's ar - chi - tec - tured by a car - ni - val of id - i - ots on

__y me in hon - or, when I'm dead __ and hit the ground, _ a love back

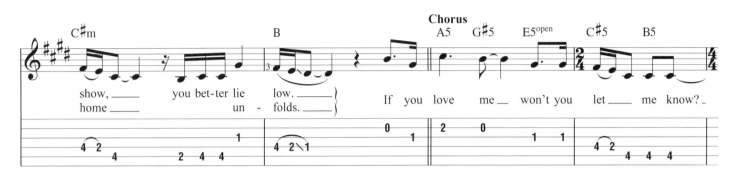

Chorus

show, ____ you bet-ter lie low. ___

home ____ un - folds. ___

If you love me _ won't you let __ me know?

1.

2. **Guitar Solo**

2. Was a long _

1.

2.

I don't wan -

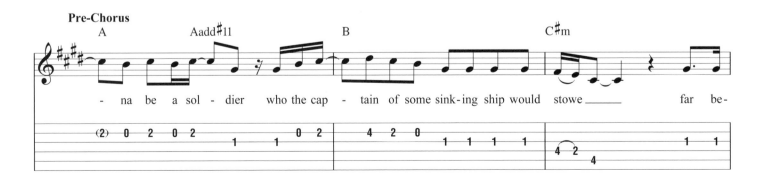

Pre-Chorus

\- na be a sol - dier who the cap - tain of some sink-ing ship would stowe _____ far be-

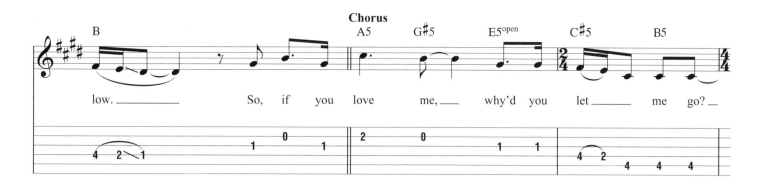

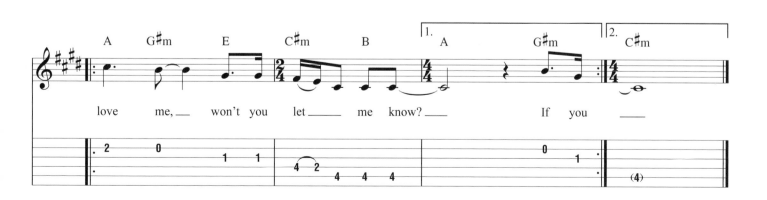

Viva la Vida

Words and Music by Guy Berryman, Jon Buckland, Will Champion and Chris Martin

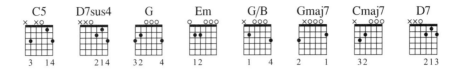

*Capo 1

Strum Pattern: 4
Pick Pattern: 5

Intro
Moderately

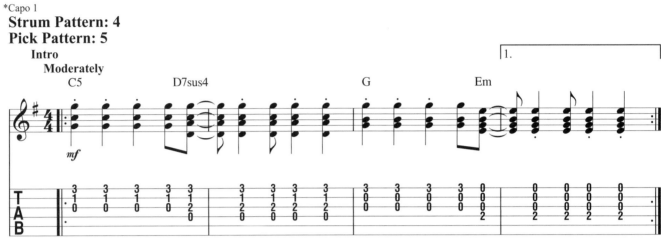

*Optional: To match recording, place capo at 1st fret.

Verse
w/ Intro pattern

1. I used to rule the world. _ Seas would rise when I gave the word. _ Now in the morn-ing I

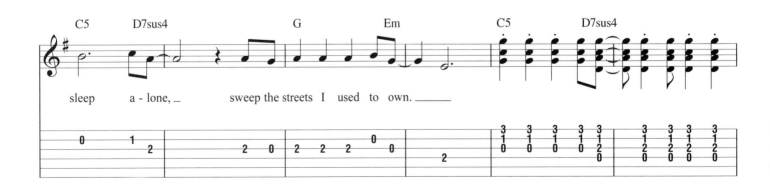

sleep a - lone, _ sweep the streets I used to own. _____

Copyright © 2008 by Universal Music Publishing MGB Ltd.
All Rights in the United States and Canada Administered by Universal Music - MGB Songs
International Copyright Secured   All Rights Reserved

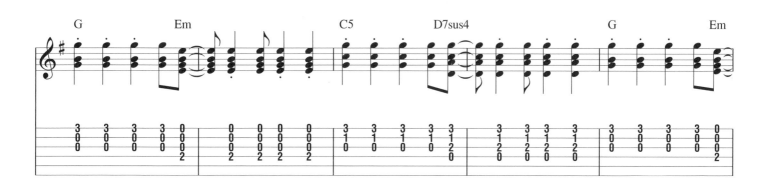

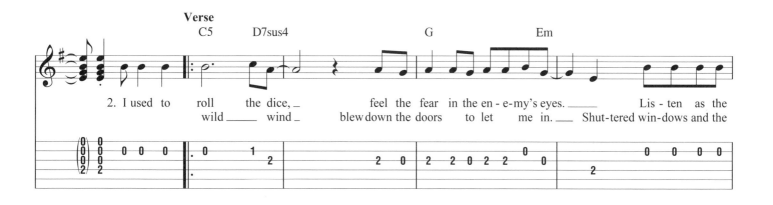

2. I used to roll the dice, feel the fear in the en - e-my's eyes. Lis - ten as the
   wild wind blew down the doors to let me in. Shut-tered win-dows and the

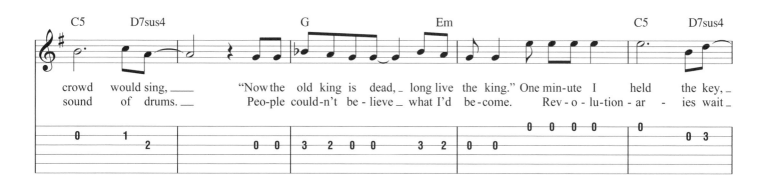

crowd would sing, "Now the old king is dead, long live the king." One min-ute I held the key,
sound of drums. Peo-ple could-n't be - lieve what I'd be-come. Rev - o - lu-tion - ar - ies wait

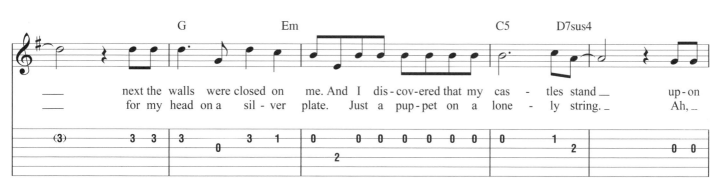

next the walls were closed on me. And I dis-cov-ered that my cas - tles stand up-on
for my head on a sil - ver plate. Just a pup-pet on a lone - ly string. Ah,

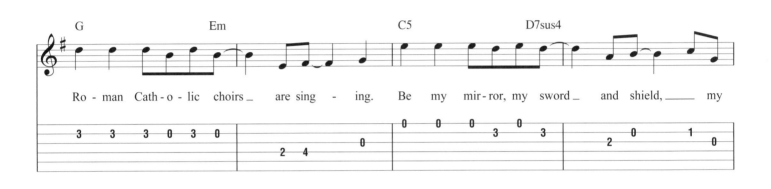

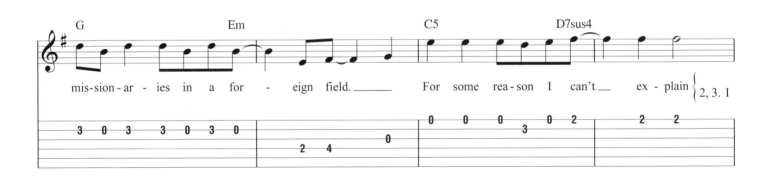

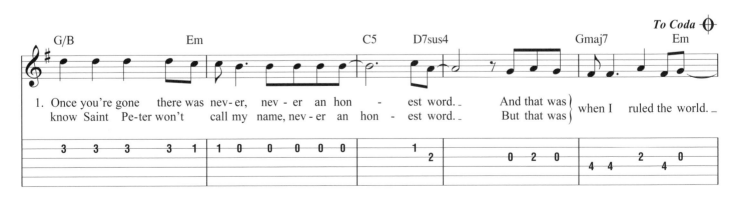

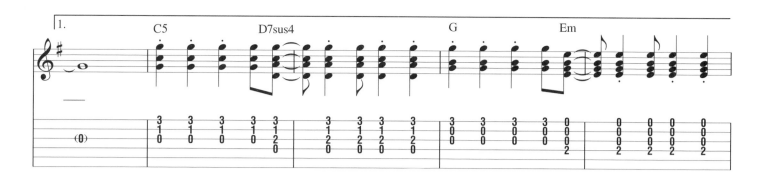

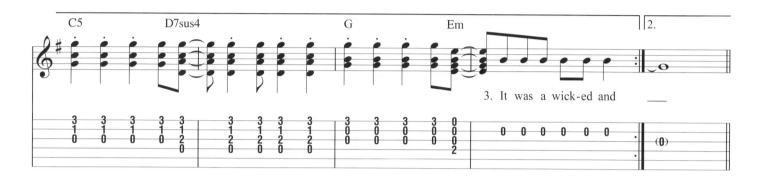

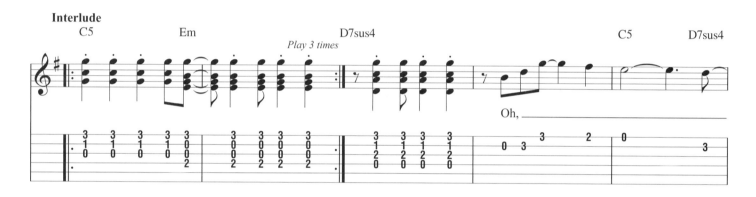

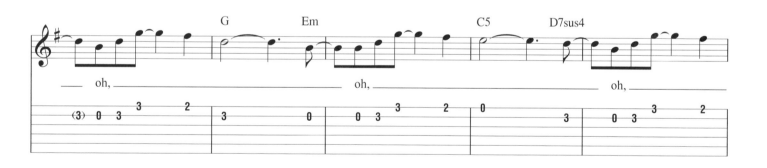

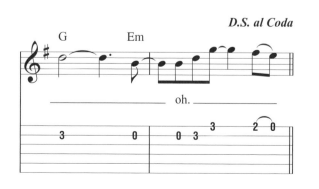

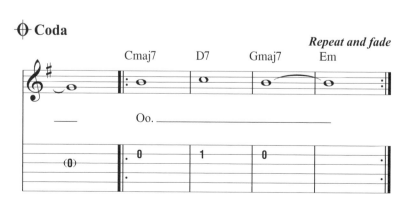

Yellow

Words and Music by Guy Berryman, Jon Buckland, Will Champion and Chris Martin

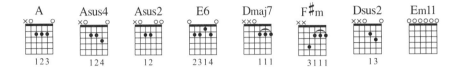

Strum Pattern: 2
Pick Pattern: 4

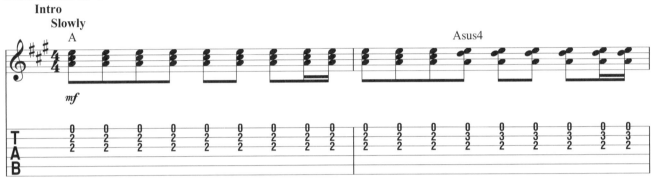

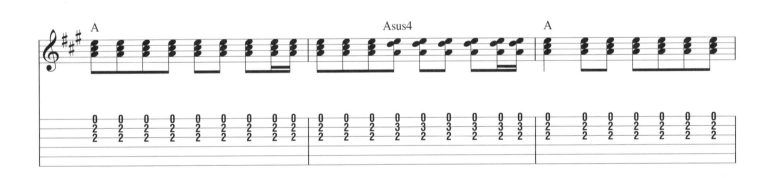

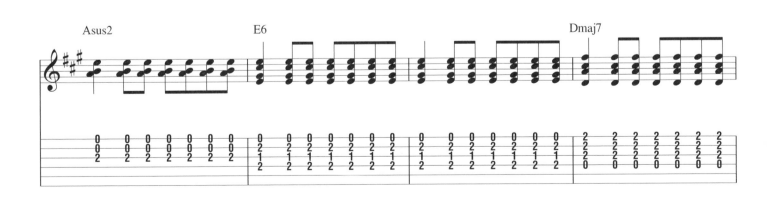

Copyright © 2000 by Universal Music Publishing MGB Ltd.
All Rights in the United States and Canada Administered by Universal Music - MGB Songs
International Copyright Secured   All Rights Reserved

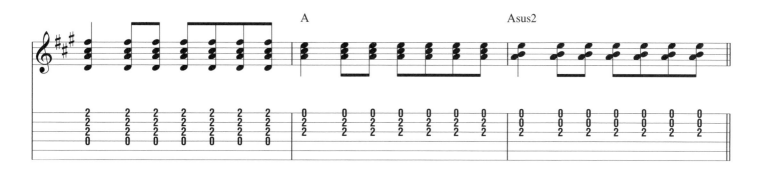

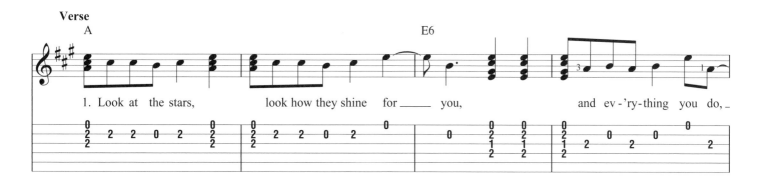

Verse

1. Look at the stars, look how they shine for _____ you, and ev-'ry-thing you do, ___

yeah, they were all ___ yel-low. ___

Verse

2. I came a - long.
3. *See additional lyrics*

I wrote a song for _____ you, and all the things you do, _____

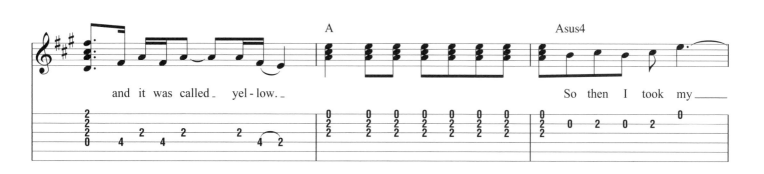

and it was called ___ yel-low. ___ So then I took my _____

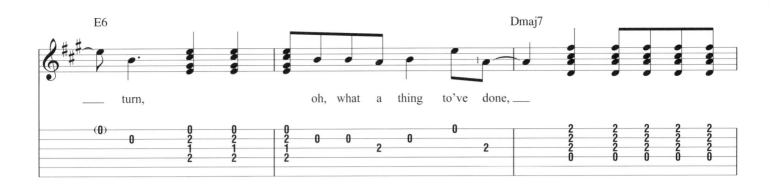

turn, oh, what a thing to've done,

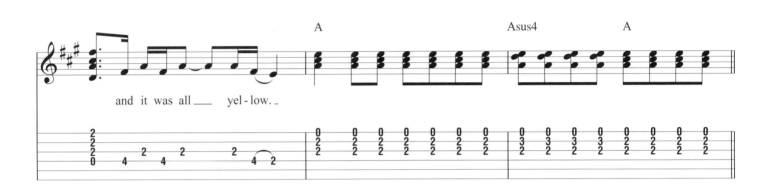

and it was all ___ yel - low.

Chorus

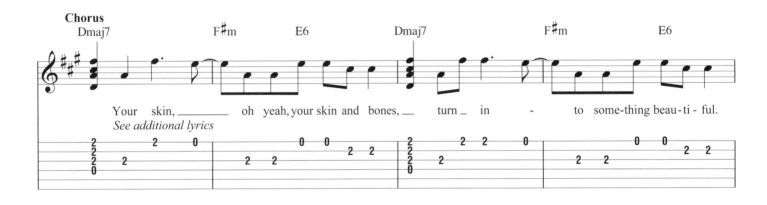

Your skin, _____ oh yeah, your skin and bones, ___ turn _ in - to some-thing beau-ti - ful.
See additional lyrics

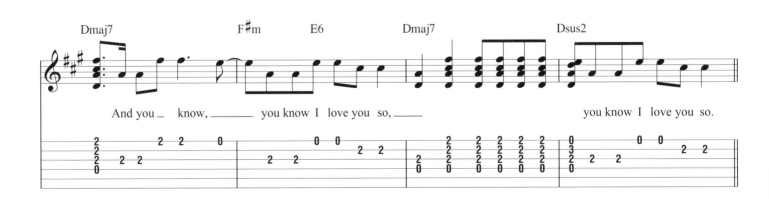

And you _ know, _____ you know I love you so, _____ you know I love you so.

Interlude

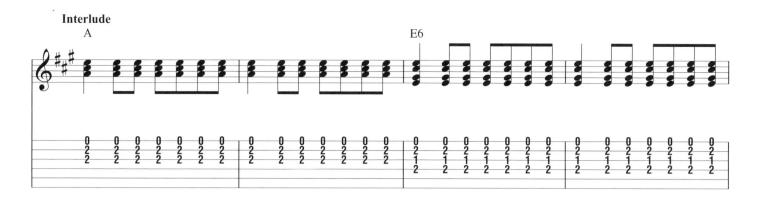

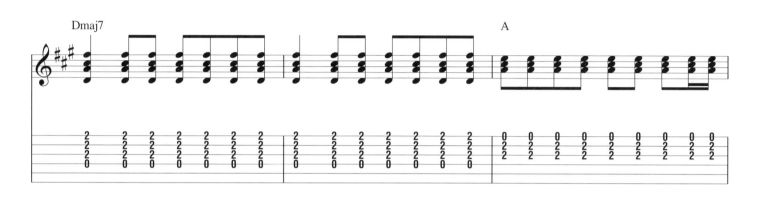

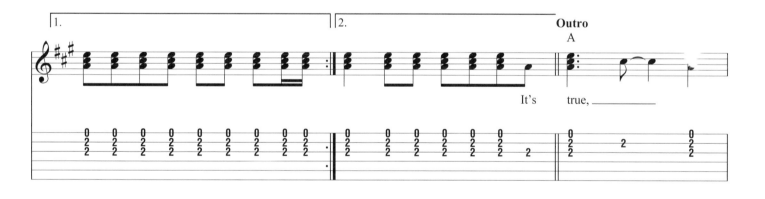

It's   true, _____

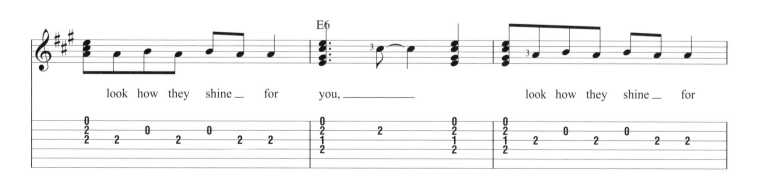

look   how   they   shine ___   for   you, _____   look   how   they   shine ___   for

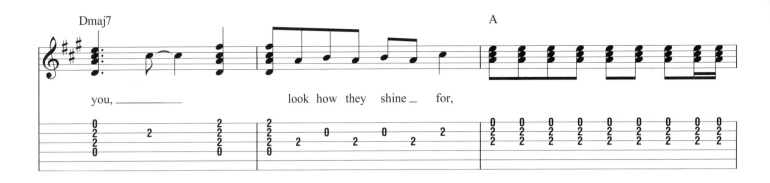

you,_____   look how they shine _ for,

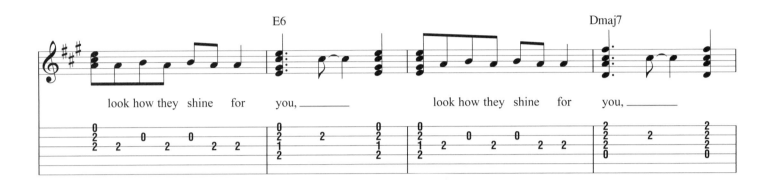

look how they shine   for   you,_____   look how they shine   for   you,_____

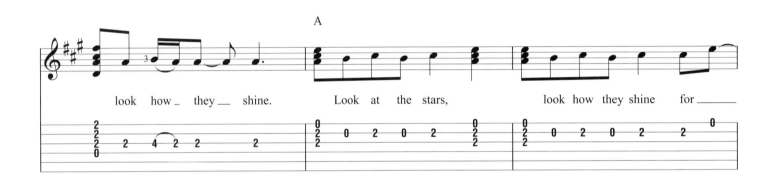

look how _ they _ shine.   Look   at   the   stars,   look how they shine   for_____

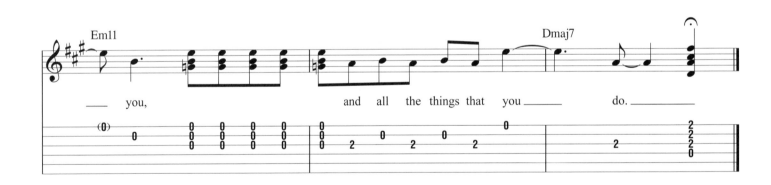

___ you,   and   all   the   things that   you_____   do. _____

Additional Lyrics

3. I swam across, I jumped for you,
   Oh, what a thing to do,
   'Cause you were all yellow. I drew a line.
   I drew a line for you,
   Oh, what a thing to do,
   And it was all yellow.

Chorus Your skin, oh yeah, your skin and bones,
          Turn into something beautiful.
          And you know, for you I'd bleed myself dry,
          For you I'd bleed myself dry.

EASY GUITAR WITH NOTES & TAB

This series features simplified arrangements with notes, tab, chord charts, and strum and pick patterns.

MIXED FOLIOS

00702287	Acoustic	$19.99
00702002	Acoustic Rock Hits for Easy Guitar	$17.99
00702166	All-Time Best Guitar Collection	$29.99
00702232	Best Acoustic Songs for Easy Guitar	$16.99
00119835	Best Children's Songs	$16.99
00703055	The Big Book of Nursery Rhymes & Children's Songs	$16.99
00698978	Big Christmas Collection	$19.99
00702394	Bluegrass Songs for Easy Guitar	$15.99
00289632	Bohemian Rhapsody	$19.99
00703387	Celtic Classics	$16.99
00224808	Chart Hits of 2016-2017	$14.99
00267383	Chart Hits of 2017-2018	$14.99
00334293	Chart Hits of 2019-2020	$16.99
00403479	Chart Hits of 2021-2022	$16.99
00702149	Children's Christian Songbook	$9.99
00702028	Christmas Classics	$9.99
00101779	Christmas Guitar	$16.99
00702141	Classic Rock	$8.95
00159642	Classical Melodies	$12.99
00253933	Disney/Pixar's Coco	$19.99
00702203	CMT's 100 Greatest Country Songs	$34.99
00702283	The Contemporary Christian Collection	$16.99
00196954	Contemporary Disney	$19.99
00702239	Country Classics for Easy Guitar	$24.99
00702257	Easy Acoustic Guitar Songs	$17.99
00702041	Favorite Hymns for Easy Guitar	$12.99
00222701	Folk Pop Songs	$19.99
00126894	Frozen	$14.99
00333922	Frozen 2	$14.99
00702286	Glee	$16.99
00702160	The Great American Country Songbook	$19.99
00702148	Great American Gospel for Guitar	$14.99
00702050	Great Classical Themes for Easy Guitar	$9.99
00148030	Halloween Guitar Songs	$17.99
00702273	Irish Songs	$14.99
00192503	Jazz Classics for Easy Guitar	$16.99
00702275	Jazz Favorites for Easy Guitar	$17.99
00702274	Jazz Standards for Easy Guitar	$19.99
00702162	Jumbo Easy Guitar Songbook	$24.99
00232285	La La Land	$16.99
00702258	Legends of Rock	$14.99
00702189	MTV's 100 Greatest Pop Songs	$34.99
00702272	1950s Rock	$16.99
00702271	1960s Rock	$16.99
00702270	1970s Rock	$24.99
00702269	1980s Rock	$16.99
00702268	1990s Rock	$24.99
00369043	Rock Songs for Kids	$14.99
00109725	Once	$14.99
00702187	Selections from O Brother Where Art Thou?	$19.99
00702178	100 Songs for Kids	$16.99
00702515	Pirates of the Caribbean	$17.99
00702125	Praise and Worship for Guitar	$14.99
00287930	Songs from *A Star Is Born, The Greatest Showman, La La Land*, and More Movie Musicals	$16.99
00702285	Southern Rock Hits	$12.99
00156420	Star Wars Music	$16.99
00121535	30 Easy Celtic Guitar Solos	$16.99
00244654	Top Hits of 2017	$14.99
00283786	Top Hits of 2018	$14.99
00302269	Top Hits of 2019	$14.99
00355779	Top Hits of 2020	$14.99
00374083	Top Hits of 2021	$16.99
00702294	Top Worship Hits	$17.99
00702255	VH1's 100 Greatest Hard Rock Songs	$39.99
00702175	VH1's 100 Greatest Songs of Rock and Roll	$34.99
00702253	Wicked	$12.99

ARTIST COLLECTIONS

00702267	AC/DC for Easy Guitar	$17.99
00156221	Adele – 25	$16.99
00396889	Adele – 30	$19.99
00702040	Best of the Allman Brothers	$16.99
00702865	J.S. Bach for Easy Guitar	$15.99
00702169	Best of The Beach Boys	$16.99
00702292	The Beatles — 1	$22.99
00125796	Best of Chuck Berry	$16.99
00702201	The Essential Black Sabbath	$15.99
00702250	blink-182 — Greatest Hits	$19.99
02501615	Zac Brown Band — The Foundation	$19.99
02501621	Zac Brown Band — You Get What You Give	$16.99
00702043	Best of Johnny Cash	$19.99
00702090	Eric Clapton's Best	$16.99
00702086	Eric Clapton — from the Album Unplugged	$17.99
00702202	The Essential Eric Clapton	$19.99
00702053	Best of Patsy Cline	$17.99
00222697	Very Best of Coldplay – 2nd Edition	$17.99
00702229	The Very Best of Creedence Clearwater Revival	$16.99
00702145	Best of Jim Croce	$16.99
00702278	Crosby, Stills & Nash	$12.99
14042809	Bob Dylan	$15.99
00702276	Fleetwood Mac — Easy Guitar Collection	$17.99
00139462	The Very Best of Grateful Dead	$17.99
00702136	Best of Merle Haggard	$19.99
00702227	Jimi Hendrix — Smash Hits	$19.99
00702288	Best of Hillsong United	$12.99
00702236	Best of Antonio Carlos Jobim	$15.99
00702245	Elton John — Greatest Hits 1970–2002	$19.99
00129855	Jack Johnson	$17.99
00702204	Robert Johnson	$16.99
00702234	Selections from Toby Keith — 35 Biggest Hits	$12.95
00702003	Kiss	$16.99
00702216	Lynyrd Skynyrd	$17.99
00702182	The Essential Bob Marley	$17.99
00146081	Maroon 5	$14.99
00121925	Bruno Mars – Unorthodox Jukebox	$12.99
00702248	Paul McCartney — All the Best	$14.99
00125484	The Best of MercyMe	$12.99
00702209	Steve Miller Band — Young Hearts (Greatest Hits)	$12.95
00124167	Jason Mraz	$15.99
00702096	Best of Nirvana	$17.99
00702211	The Offspring — Greatest Hits	$17.99
00138026	One Direction	$17.99
00702030	Best of Roy Orbison	$17.99
00702144	Best of Ozzy Osbourne	$14.99
00702279	Tom Petty	$17.99
00102911	Pink Floyd	$17.99
00702139	Elvis Country Favorites	$19.99
00702293	The Very Best of Prince	$22.99
00699415	Best of Queen for Guitar	$16.99
00109279	Best of R.E.M.	$14.99
00702208	Red Hot Chili Peppers — Greatest Hits	$19.99
00198960	The Rolling Stones	$17.99
00174793	The Very Best of Santana	$16.99
00702196	Best of Bob Seger	$16.99
00146046	Ed Sheeran	$19.99
00702252	Frank Sinatra — Nothing But the Best	$12.99
00702010	Best of Rod Stewart	$17.99
00702049	Best of George Strait	$17.99
00702259	Taylor Swift for Easy Guitar	$15.99
00359800	Taylor Swift – Easy Guitar Anthology	$24.99
00702260	Taylor Swift — Fearless	$14.99
00139727	Taylor Swift – 1989	$19.99
00115960	Taylor Swift — Red	$16.99
00253667	Taylor Swift — Reputation	$17.99
00702290	Taylor Swift — Speak Now	$16.99
00232849	Chris Tomlin Collection – 2nd Edition	$14.99
00702226	Chris Tomlin — See the Morning	$12.95
00148643	Train	$14.99
00702427	U2 — 18 Singles	$19.99
00702108	Best of Stevie Ray Vaughan	$17.99
00279005	The Who	$14.99
00702123	Best of Hank Williams	$15.99
00194548	Best of John Williams	$14.99
00702228	Neil Young — Greatest Hits	$17.99
00119133	Neil Young — Harvest	$16.99

Prices, contents and availability subject to change without notice.

HAL•LEONARD®

Visit Hal Leonard online at halleonard.com

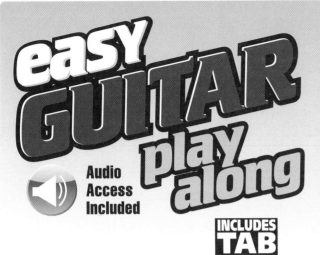

easy GUITAR play along

Audio Access Included

INCLUDES TAB

The *Easy Guitar Play Along®* series features streamlined transcriptions of your favorite songs. Just follow the tab, listen to the audio to hear how the guitar should sound, and then play along using the backing tracks. Playback tools are provided for slowing down the tempo without changing pitch and looping challenging parts. The melody and lyrics are included in the book so that you can sing or simply follow along.

1. ROCK CLASSICS

Jailbreak • Living After Midnight • Mississippi Queen • Rocks Off • Runnin' Down a Dream • Smoke on the Water • Strutter • Up Around the Bend.

00702560 Book/CD Pack....... $14.99

2. ACOUSTIC TOP HITS

About a Girl • I'm Yours • The Lazy Song • The Scientist • 21 Guns • Upside Down • What I Got • Wonderwall.

00702569 Book/CD Pack....... $14.99

3. ROCK HITS

All the Small Things • Best of You • Brain Stew (The Godzilla Remix) • Californication • Island in the Sun • Plush • Smells Like Teen Spirit • Use Somebody.

00702570 Book/CD Pack....... $14.99

4. ROCK 'N' ROLL

Blue Suede Shoes • I Get Around • I'm a Believer • Jailhouse Rock • Oh, Pretty Woman • Peggy Sue • Runaway • Wake Up Little Susie.

00702572 Book/CD Pack....... $14.99

6. CHRISTMAS SONGS

Have Yourself a Merry Little Christmas • A Holly Jolly Christmas • The Little Drummer Boy • Run Rudolph Run • Santa Claus Is Comin' to Town • Silver and Gold • Sleigh Ride • Winter Wonderland.

00101879 Book/CD Pack......... $14.99

7. BLUES SONGS FOR BEGINNERS

Come On (Part 1) • Double Trouble • Gangster of Love • I'm Ready • Let Me Love You Baby • Mary Had a Little Lamb • San-Ho-Zay • T-Bone Shuffle.

00103235 Book/
　　　　Online Audio..........$17.99

9. ROCK SONGS FOR BEGINNERS

Are You Gonna Be My Girl • Buddy Holly • Everybody Hurts • In Bloom • Otherside • The Rock Show • Santa Monica • When I Come Around.

00103255 Book/CD Pack.....$14.99

10. GREEN DAY

Basket Case • Boulevard of Broken Dreams • Good Riddance (Time of Your Life) • Holiday • Longview • 21 Guns • Wake Me up When September Ends • When I Come Around.

00122322 Book/
　　　　Online Audio........$16.99

11. NIRVANA

All Apologies • Come As You Are • Heart Shaped Box • Lake of Fire • Lithium • The Man Who Sold the World • Rape Me • Smells Like Teen Spirit.

00122325 Book/
　　　　Online Audio........ $17.99

13. AC/DC

Back in Black • Dirty Deeds Done Dirt Cheap • For Those About to Rock (We Salute You) • Hells Bells • Highway to Hell • Rock and Roll Ain't Noise Pollution • T.N.T. • You Shook Me All Night Long.

14042895 Book/
　　　　Online Audio........ $17.99

14. JIMI HENDRIX – SMASH HITS

All Along the Watchtower • Can You See Me • Crosstown Traffic • Fire • Foxey Lady • Hey Joe • Manic Depression • Purple Haze • Red House • Remember • Stone Free • The Wind Cries Mary.

00130591 Book/
　　　　Online Audio........$24.99

HAL•LEONARD®

www.halleonard.com

Prices, contents, and availability subject to change without notice.